Living *Water*

Treasure Seekers

Living Water

a creative resource for the Liturgy

Treasure Seekers
YEAR C

Susan Sayers
with Father Andrew Moore

Illustrated by Arthur Baker

Kevin Mayhew

First published in 2000 by
KEVIN MAYHEW LTD
Buxhall
Stowmarket
Suffolk IP14 3BW

0 1 2 3 4 5 6 7 8 9

ISBN 1 84003 516 1
Catalogue No. 1500341

The other titles in the *Living Water* series are

Complete Resource Book	ISBN 1 84003 513 7	Cat. No. 1500340
Prayer of the Faithful	ISBN 1 84003 553 6	Cat. No. 1500355
Pearl Divers	ISBN 1 84003 515 3	Cat. No. 1500342
Gold Panners	ISBN 1 84003 514 5	Cat. No. 1500343

Cover photographs:
Two small children – courtesy of SuperStock Ltd, London
Background – courtesy of Images Colour Library Ltd, London
Cover design by Jaquetta Sergeant
Edited by Katherine Laidler
Typesetting by Louise Selfe
Printed in Great Britain

FOREWORD

For this age group the world is opening out from the immediate family circle, and full of possibilities. The children are becoming aware of familiar faces Sunday by Sunday. It can be a daunting prospect, and the way young children are met and welcomed, talked and listened to, when they first encounter the children's liturgy in your church, will have a profound effect on their spiritual growth. It is through the good humour, care and friendliness of those they meet that they will begin to realise how God loves them.

In all your planning, keep aware of how it will seem from the children's point of view. Is the area attractive and inviting? Does the furniture fit? Is the atmosphere orderly and therefore unthreatening? Are people talking at a speed they can cope with, and giving them time to reply without pressure? Do people genuinely seem to like them and want them to be happy? Is considerate love and fairness expressed in actions as well as in the teaching? Is it a place where they can relax and feel at home? Is it fun?

These things are so important because the children will be learning far more from the way things are done and from the people they work with, than from the actual teaching content, valuable as this obviously is. It is a good idea to review your aims and objectives annually, setting out for yourselves, the parents, and any helpers, what you are doing and why, what works well and what needs to be tried differently. If this regular review is built into the system there is no danger of outdated methods carrying on past their sell-by date just because things have always been done like that. A termly or annual training day is also helpful in refreshing leaders and preventing cases of burn-out.

This book provides you with ideas and materials for activities for young children, all based on the weekly Lectionary readings. The activity sheets often include something to think and talk about together, and you can select and adapt the ideas to suit your particular group. Vary the media the children work with – crayons, finger paints, sponge painting, printing, paper and fabric collage, chalks and pastels are all fun to use. Pray for the children and their families, and read the Bible passages before you plan, so as to incorporate your own valuable insights, and use the suggested games either as they stand or as starting points to help you think of other ideas of your own.

A few general ideas about story-telling:

- Tell the story from the viewpoint of a character in the situation. To create the time-machine effect, avoid eye contact as you slowly put on the appropriate cloth or cloak, and then make eye contact as you greet the children in character.
- Have an object with you which leads into the story – a water jug, or a lunch box, for instance.
- Walk the whole group through the story, so that they are physically moving from one place to another; and use all kinds of places, such as broom cupboards, under the stairs, outside under the trees, and so on.

- Collect some carpet tiles – blue and green – so that at story time the children can sit round the edge of this and help you place on the cut-outs for the story.

If parents are going to be staying with their children, involve them in the activities, or think over the possibility of having an adult discussion group in the same room, using the study material and discussion questions in the *Living Water* Complete Resource Book. Parents are encouraged to pray with their children during the week, using the worksheet prayers.

All the material in the book is copyright-free for non-commercial use in churches and schools.

SUSAN SAYERS
with Father Andrew Moore

CONTENTS

Teaching programmes and activity sheets for the following Special Feasts will be found in the *Treasure Seekers* book for Year A.

Mary, Mother of God – 1 January
The Presentation of the Lord (Candlemas) – 2 February
Saint John the Baptist – 24 June
Saints Peter and Paul – 29 June
The Transfiguration of the Lord – 6 August
The Assumption – 15 August
The Triumph of the Holy Cross – 14 September
All Saints – 1 November
Feasts of the Dedication of a Church

This book is dedicated to my family and friends,
whose encouraging support has been wonderful,
and to all those whose good ideas are included here for others to share.

RECOMMENDED BIBLES

It is often a good idea to look at a passage in several different versions before deciding which to use for a particular occasion.

As far as children are concerned, separate Bible stories, such as those published by Palm Tree Press and Lion, are a good introduction for the very young. Once children are reading, a very helpful version is the *International Children's Bible* (New Century version) published by Word Publishing. Here children have a translation based on experienced scholarship, using language structure suitable for young readers, with short sentences and appropriate vocabulary. There is a helpful dictionary, and clear maps and pictures are provided.

ADVENT

First Sunday of Advent

Thought for the day

The gathered hopes of generations remind us to get ourselves ready, so that Christ's return will be a day of excitement and great joy.

Readings

Jeremiah 33:14-16
Psalm 24
1 Thessalonians 3:12-4:2
Luke 21:25-28, 34-36

Aim

To help them understand getting ready for Christmas in terms of getting ready to meet Jesus in person.

Starter

Stop . . . Get ready . . . Go! Starting always from standing still in a space on their own, on the word 'Go!' the children do whatever the leader calls out (e.g. hop like rabbits, swim around like fish, slither like snakes). When the leader calls 'Stop!' the children stop and at 'Get ready!' they go to the starting position again.

Teaching

Draw their attention to the way they had to get ready for the game each time. Christmas is coming – whose birthday is it at Christmas? How are we going to get ready for Christmas?

Jesus told us that one day he would come back. We will be able to see him, either then or when we die, whichever happens first.

How can we get ready to meet Jesus? What would he like to see us doing?

During the discussion, make simple drawings of the way they think Jesus would like to see them living.

Praying

The children find a space on their own again. Taking the ideas they have come up with, lead the children to pray: 'Jesus, we want to be ready to meet you. Please help us to . . . (share our toys/forgive each other/be kind to our brothers and sisters, etc.)', and everyone mimes the activity. Then call out 'Stop!' and the children go back to their space for the next prayer.

Activities

Use the worksheet to reinforce the idea of getting ready for Christmas being linked with getting ready to meet Jesus.

Notes

Here I am getting ready for Christmas.
4 3 2 1
Weeks to Christmas
Here I am getting ready for Jesus.
Jesus is coming
Get ready to paint!
We are starting to make a Christmas crib today.
You will need a box.
a brush
some brown paint
POSTER COLOUR
For parents and children together. This week's prayer
Dear Jesus, thank you for loving us so much. Amen.
Next week we will make the manger.

Second Sunday of Advent

Thought for the day

It had been prophesied that there would be a messenger to prepare the way for the coming of the Messiah. Now John the Baptist appears with his urgent message of repentance.

Readings

Baruch 5:1-9
Psalm 125
Philippians 1:3-6, 8-11
Luke 3:1-6

Aim

To understand that John was the messenger helping people get ready for Jesus.

Starter

Call and change. Sit round in a circle. One person calls someone else's name and these two change places. The one who was called becomes the next caller. This game helps build the group together, and is an acting-out of what John the Baptist was doing.

Teaching

Find out if any of the children have cousins, and what their names are. Point out that they may not live with you but they are members of your family.

Tell them that one of Jesus' cousins was John. And God had a job he needed John to do. When John was grown up God asked him to go and get people ready for Jesus.

How could he do that? First he went off on his own to pray. Then he started talking to the people. He said to them, 'Listen, I've got a message for you!'

'A message for us?' asked the people. 'What message have you got for us?'

'Well,' said John, 'we all need to get ready. Soon God will be coming to us, and we aren't ready for him yet.'

'How exciting!' said the people. 'You are right, we must be ready to welcome him. But what can we do?'

John said, 'God will want to find that we are kind and loving and being fair to one another.'

'Oh dear!' said the people. 'I'm afraid we're not always like that. Some of us have bad tempers and some of us are greedy and some of us want our own way all the time. But we do want to be ready. Please help us get ready.'

'All you have to do,' said John, 'is to be sorry about those things and want to put them right.'

'We are sorry,' said the people. 'We don't want to be bad tempered and greedy and wanting our own way all the time. We want to make God happy when he comes.'

'In that case,' said John, 'I will wash you in the river as a sign that your bad temper and greediness and wanting your own way all the time are washed away and you are forgiven.'

The people felt happy and free. They went back home to enjoy loving and sharing and being fair. It would not be easy, but they were determined to do their best.

Praying

Ask the children to sit with their hands closed up as if they are hiding something inside. Imagine that one hand holds something for which you want to thank God that you are good at. As you open that hand, think of showing the thing you are good at to God. Everyone says, 'Thank you, God, for making me good at this.' Imagine that in the other hand you are holding something you would like to be better at (telling the truth/being a good friend/helping at home). As you open this hand, think of showing God and say, 'Please, God, help me to be better at this.'

Activities

Use the worksheet to continue getting the crib ready for Christmas – today is the manger – and reinforce the teaching about John the Baptist.

Notes

Jesus and John were cousins and played together.

'Your life is washed clean.'

Weeks to Christmas

John helps us to get ready

We are getting our Christmas crib ready. You will need

- [ ] crayons
- [ ] a box
- [ ] yellow paper
- [ ] scissors

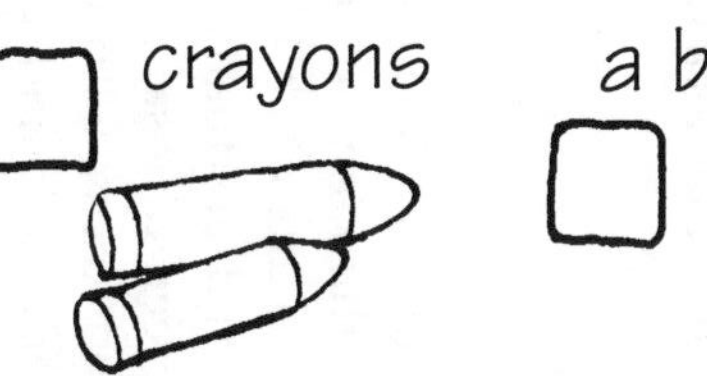

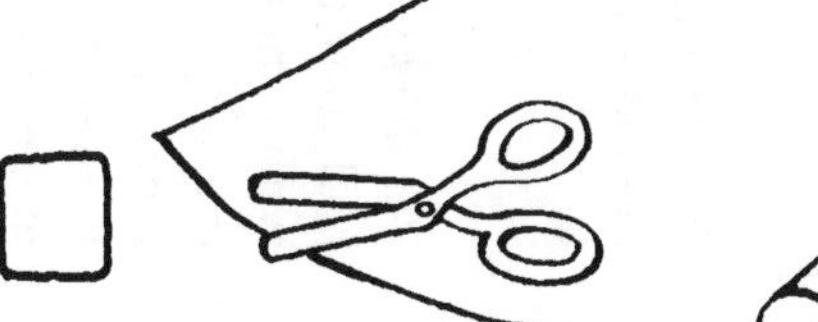

- Colour the box brown.
- Cut the paper into strips of hay and fill the manger.

Parents and children together at home.

A prayer when you open each Advent calendar window.

Dear God, thank you for loving us so much. Amen.

Third Sunday of Advent

Thought for the day

Our period of preparation shifts from repentance and forgiveness to the freed exhilaration of hope, as the momentous truth of God's immanence begins to dawn on us.

Readings

Zephaniah 3:14-18
Canticle: Isaiah 12:2-6
Philippians 4:4-7
Luke 3:10-18

Aim

To celebrate looking forward to Christmas as a time of God's love being shown to us.

Starter

I'm thinking of someone . . . Everyone sits in a circle and tries to guess who you are thinking of. Start with something that could refer to lots of children (he's a boy/wearing a sweater) and gradually get more specific (his shoes have green dinosaurs on the bottom) until lots of children know who you mean. Everyone says, 'God made Jack and God loves Jack.'

Teaching

Beforehand get a good quality picture of the nativity (from a Christmas card) and put it in a box. Wrap the box in Christmas paper. We will use this during the teaching.

Get out some wrapping paper and scissors, and let the children guess what they are used for. Talk about why we give each other presents at Christmas, and establish that it isn't because we want something back but because we love the people and want them to see that we love them.

Now remind them of the starter activity and how God knows and loves each of us. Explain that at the first Christmas he gave the world the best Christmas present ever, not because he wanted anything back, but just because he loves us so much. Show the Christmas present. What was God's Christmas present to the world, to show he loves us? Open the present and let the children see that it is Jesus.

Praying

As you hold the Christmas present and then open it and hold up the picture, say this prayer together:

Thank you, God,
for loving the world so much
that you gave us Jesus
to be with us for ever. Amen.

Activities

Use the worksheet to continue getting ready for Christmas by making the crib – this week it's Mary, Joseph and Jesus. The present-wrapping activity will need a variety of small pieces of Christmas paper.

Notes

We are getting ready for Christmas!
You will need
glue
crayons
scissors
At home . . .
Thank you, God, for loving the world so much that you gave us Jesus to be with us for ever.
Amen.
Colour Mary, Joseph and Jesus.
Cut them out.
Stick them on the wall.
Weeks to Christmas
4 3 2 1
We give presents to show we love someone.
Can you wrap these presents?
Jesus

Fourth Sunday of Advent

Thought for the day

When we co-operate with God amazing things happen.

Readings

Micah 5:1-4
Psalm 79
Hebrews 10:5-10
Luke 1:39-44

Aim

To understand that Mary was happy to work with God.

Starter

Working together. Ask the children to help you do various jobs as you get ready for the session. If you have access to a parachute, play some parachute games which need everyone to work together (such as 'mushroom', 'roll the ball' or tent making). Alternatively have everyone helping to make a 'Happy Christmas' frieze for the church.

Teaching

Point out how we all worked together in that activity. What jobs do they help with at home? Each time emphasise the co-operation that gets the job done well.

Use rag dolls or cut-out figures to tell the story.

God needed a very important job done. He needed someone to bring Jesus into our world and look after him. So he looked around and saw just the right person: Mary. He didn't choose her because she was rich or pretty or clever. He chose her because she was ready to work with God. She was already friends with him. She talked to him and listened to him in her prayers each day, and tried to live as God wanted her to. (How was that?)

So one day God told her he had chosen her to be the mother of Jesus. Mary was very surprised. It was such an important job, and she knew it would be a hard job to do well. What do you think – did she say yes or no?

Mary said 'Yes!' and went off to visit her cousin Elizabeth who lived in another town. Elizabeth was going to have a baby, too. You remember John the Baptist we met last week? Well, it was him, only he hadn't been born yet when Mary went to see his mother.

As soon as they met they hugged and kissed, and John started leaping about inside his mum because he was so excited! (Have you ever felt a baby moving about inside your mum? It's a funny feeling.)

Mary didn't need to tell Elizabeth her news. Elizabeth seemed to know already, and they sang and danced to praise God for being so wonderful.

Praying

Leader Dear God,
when you want us to be kind, help us to say

All Yes!

Leader When you want us to be honest, help us to say

All Yes!

Leader When you want us to help someone, help us to say

All Yes!

Activities

The worksheet helps the children to complete their Christmas crib today, so these can be blessed in church and taken home. They are also going over the main points of today's story.

Notes

We are getting ready for Christmas!
yellow paper
lolly stick
star
scissors
glue
sticky tape
Please come!
Thank you for coming Jesus
Elizabeth
Mary
Weeks to Christmas
4 3 2 1
A prayer to say before Christmas dinner
Thank you, Lord God, for all the food and the love we share.
Amen.

CHRISTMAS

CHRISTMAS DAY

Thought for the day

Emmanuel – 'God with us' – is born at Bethlehem into the human family. Now we will be able to understand, in human terms, what God is really like.

Readings

Note: These readings are for Midnight Mass. Readings for the Day Mass are to be found in *Living Water* Year A, and for the Mass at Dawn in *Living Water* Year B.

Isaiah 9:2-7
Psalm 97
Titus 2:11-14
Luke 2:1-14 (15-20)

Activities

Christmas Day is very much a time for all God's children to worship together.

Involve all the children in the singing and playing of carols, decorating the church, and in the other ministries of welcoming, serving, collection of gifts and so on. Have nativity toys for the very young to play with, such as knitted Mary, Joseph and Jesus, sheep and shepherds.

A colouring activity for today is provided.

Notes

Jesus is born!

First Sunday of Christmas: The Holy Family

Thought for the day

Jesus' perception and understanding of his purpose and work begins to take shape throughout his childhood.

Readings

Ecclesiasticus 3:2-6, 12-14
Psalm 127
Colossians 3:12-21
Luke 2:41-52

Aim

To get to know the story of Jesus being lost and found.

Starter

Play hide and seek in small groups so that everyone gets the chance both to hide and be found.

Teaching

Talk about how it felt to be looking for the hidden children and how it felt to find them. Today's story is about a time when Mary and Joseph went looking for Jesus.

Using the 'carpet tiles and cut-outs' method tell the story of the visit to Jerusalem with all the mums and dads and children and uncles and aunties and grandparents and cousins. Jesus was twelve years old. Give all the children a cut-out donkey or camel to add to the trail of visitors going up to Jerusalem. Pictures to use in the story are given with the worksheet.

When everyone sets off for home all the trail of animals can be turned over to face the other way, and then Mary and Joseph's donkey will turn back again to find Jesus, before finally joining the others.

Praying

When we are sitting still *(sit still)*:
we know you are with us, Jesus.
When we are walking along *(walk along)*:
we know you are with us, Jesus.
When we are playing *(play)*:
we know you are with us, Jesus.
When we are helping *(pretend to help clean or tidy up)*:
we know you are with us, Jesus. Amen.

Activities

The worksheet has a searching to find activity and consolidates the main points of the story. The children can also talk over what to do if they ever lose their mum or dad when they are out shopping.

Notes

Jesus is lost . . .

Can you see them?

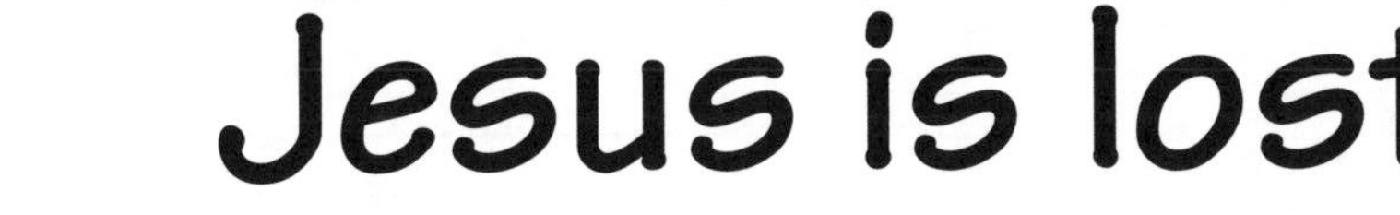

Stick the picture of Jesus where Mary and Joseph found him in the end.

. . . and found

Cut out Jesus. Where did Mary and Joseph find him?

For parents

Your child has been thinking about what to do if they get lost. Can you fill in the details that apply in your particular family?

To pray together

When we are sitting still (sit still)
we know you are with us, Jesus.
When we are walking along (walk along)
we know you are with us, Jesus.

(Add other verses like brushing our teeth, driving to Nana's, shopping, cleaning the car, etc.)

SECOND SUNDAY OF CHRISTMAS

Thought for the day

Christ is the way God tells people about himself.

Readings

Sirach 24:1-4, 12-16
Psalm 147
Ephesians 1:3-6, 15-18
John 1:1-18

Aim

To help them understand that God shows us he loves us by coming to live with us.

Starter

Have some raisins or chocolate buttons which you hand round to each child in turn, by name. Point out that you are fond of them, and wanted to show them by giving them a little something. God loves each of us by name, and he had a very good idea for showing us his love.

Teaching

One day God was looking at all the world he had made. He smelt the roses, laughed at the monkeys playing in the trees, smiled to himself as a child helped his baby brother to play football, and enjoyed the beautiful sunset. It was a very good world.

Then he got sad as he watched an owner hitting a dog, two children fighting, and a grown-up stealing some money. God had made people able to choose right or wrong, and lots of them were choosing wrong instead of right, even though God knew it would make them happier to choose right.

The trouble was that although he was there, the people couldn't see him. No one can see God. And God longed to help them.

One day he decided to become a human himself and live among them. 'And then,' thought God, 'they will understand how to live. They will be able to follow my example, and I will help them.'

Well, of course God couldn't stop being God and be a human instead – if he did that all the world would come to a sudden and nasty end.

So this is what God did. He spoke his great love for the world and his longing for the people, and the great love he spoke became a human baby, all ready to grow up in a human family, and show all the people what God was really like.

And do you know the name of that baby, born from the word of great love that God spoke? The baby's name was Jesus, and we have just been celebrating his birthday! Jesus is God saying 'I love you'.

Praying

Jesus, you show us what God is like.
You show us that he loves us.
Thank you, Jesus! Amen.

Activities

On the worksheet there are instructions for making a frame to put on a mirror. Whoever looks into the mirror will see someone God loves. There is also a dot-to-dot which helps us see something we couldn't see before and a picture which reinforces the teaching.

Notes

Who is hidden here? Join the dots to see it.

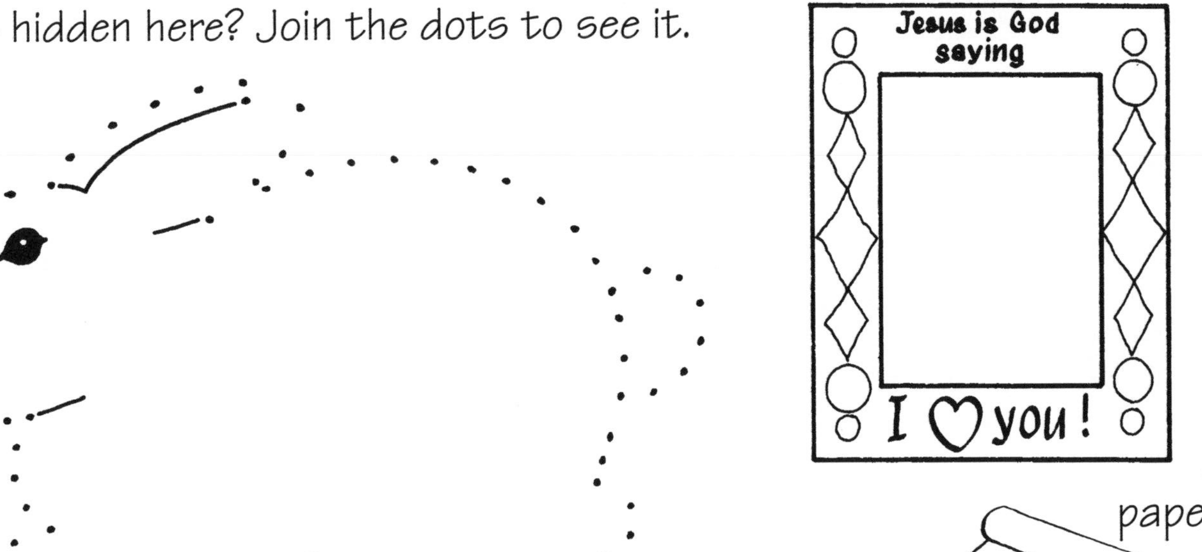

1 Colour the frame
2 Cut out the middle
3 Stick it on shiny mirror paper
4 Let your family and friends look in it

You will need

glue

crayons

scissors

paper

For parents

Look for things God has made which are good/faithful.

Read some stories of Jesus.

Pray with your child.

God is hidden, too. But we can see him in Jesus.

Jesus, you show us what God is like.
You show us that he loves us.
Thank you, Jesus.
Amen.

THE EPIPHANY OF THE LORD

Thought for the day

Jesus, the hope of the nations, is shown to the world.

Readings

Isaiah 60:1-6
Psalm 71
Ephesians 3:2-3a, 5-6
Matthew 2:1-12

Aim

To become familiar with the story of the wise men finding Jesus.

Starter

Play pass the parcel. At the different layers have old bus and train tickets. The prize at the end is a star-shaped biscuit.

Teaching

Tell the children that today we are going to hear about a journey. It isn't a bus journey or a car journey or a train journey. This is a camel journey. (All pack your bags and get on your camels.) We are very wise people, but we don't know where we are going. We are looking for a baby king. And we are packing presents for him. (Pack gold, frankincense and myrrh.) Produce a star on a stick as you explain how a special star has started shining in the sky and we are sure it will lead us to the baby king. Lead off behind the star, riding your camels, and pretending to go over high mountains, through water, stopping for the night, and going to sleep and so on. At last you reach the town of Bethlehem (stick up a sign) where you find the baby king with his mum and dad. (Have a large picture, or one of the cribs made before Christmas.) We all get off our camels and give the baby our presents. The baby's name is Jesus and we have found him at last!

Praying

This is a prayer the wise men might have said. We have all been invited to find Jesus as well, so we can say it with them.

Thank you, Jesus,
for inviting me
to come and look for you.
I am glad I have found you! Amen.

Activities

To emphasise that the journey of the wise men was probably a hard one, there is a maze to help the wise men find their way to Bethlehem. The star-making activity will need star templates, and ready-cut card for the younger children.

Notes

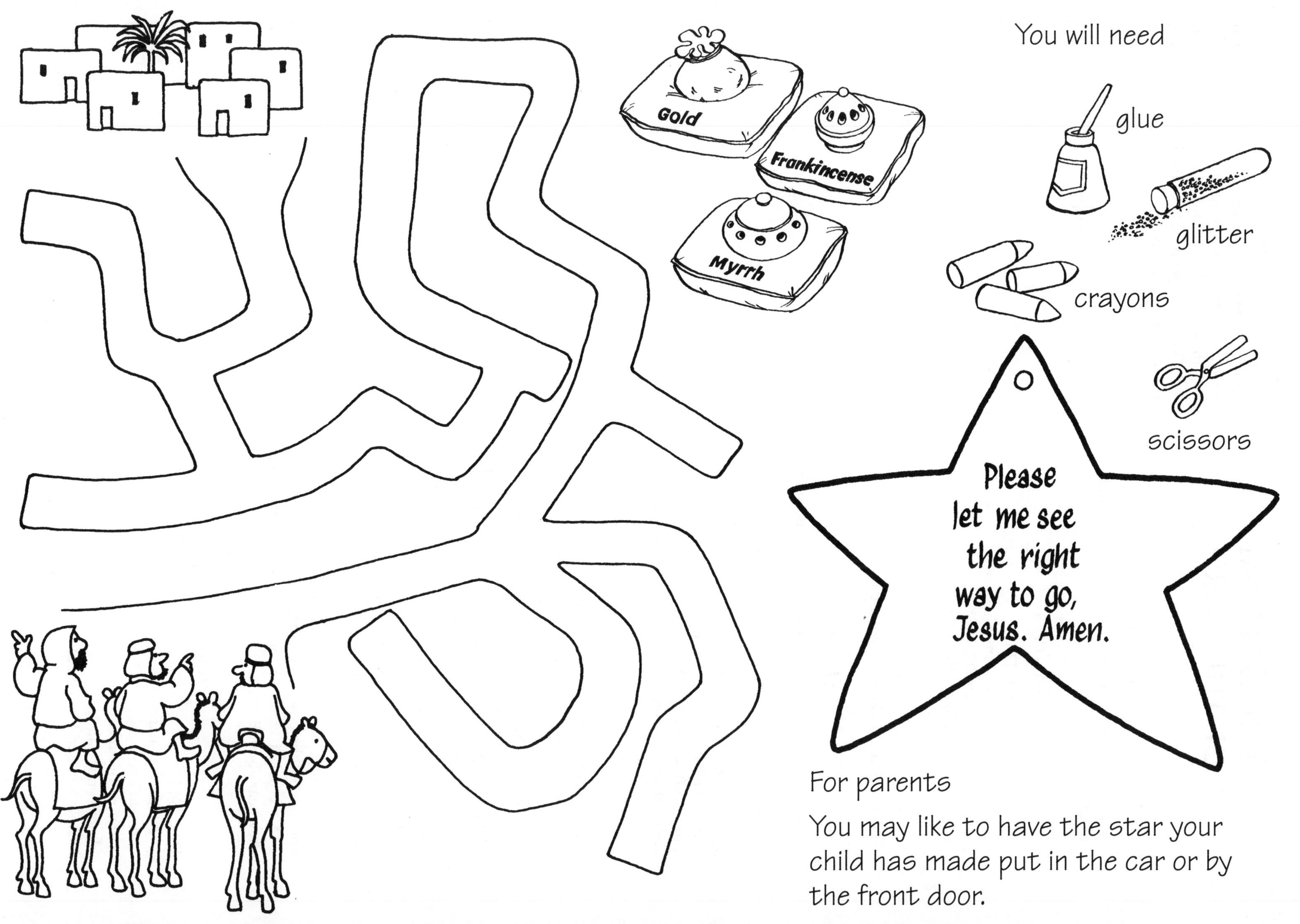

For parents

You may like to have the star your child has made put in the car or by the front door.

THE BAPTISM OF THE LORD

Thought for the day

Jesus is baptised, and God confirms his identity and his calling.

Readings

Isaiah 42:1-4, 6-7
Psalm 28
Acts 10:34-38
Luke 3:15-16, 21-22

Aim

To know that God knows them by name.

Starter

Have a number of pictures or objects set out in the middle of the circle. The children guess the name you are thinking of by the way you describe the object or picture. Start with more general statements and get more specific, like this: 'I'm thinking of something which is round . . . and white . . . and you might put cornflakes in it.' They have to say the name, rather than pointing, unless they are very young.

Teaching

Have the children's names written out carefully on cards with a string attached so they can be worn. Hold up each one in turn and describe the person the name belongs to, by nature as well as looks, and with lots of positives. The children can join in by adding things they like about each one. When all the children are wearing their names, tell them how God knows each of us by name. He already knows all the things about us that we have talked about, and lots more as well.

Show a picture of a baby, a child, and an adult being baptised, and talk about God calling us by name to follow him. They may remember a Baptism in the family, or one of the recent ones in church, and can tell the others what happened. Have a jug and a bowl of water so they can focus on that as they hear about Baptism.

Praying

Dear God,
you know my name
and you know me
and you love me.
I know your name.
I know you and I love you!

Activities

The name cards can be decorated with coloured sticky paper, finger-painting or with pens. On the sheet there are objects and people to name, and thank God for, and space to draw themselves doing something they like doing.

Notes

Can you name these?

To pray with your child

**Dear God,
you know my name
and you know me
and you love me.
I know your name.
I know you and
I love you!**

LENT

First Sunday of Lent

Thought for the day

Following his baptism, Jesus is severely tempted out in the desert, and shows us how to overcome temptation.

Readings

Deuteronomy 26:4-10
Psalm 90
Romans 10:8b-13
Luke 4:1-13

Aim

To look at good ways of living.

Starter

Have a selection of balancing activities for the children to try. These could include walking between two chalk-drawn lines, climbing up to stand on a chair without using your hands, walking along a bench, standing on one leg, and walking along a piece of string laid along the floor.

Teaching

Talk about the balancing acts and how we had to try hard to stop ourselves falling and to keep our balance. In the way we live we have to try hard to do what is kind and loving and good. (Walk along the string line as you say this.) Sometimes we fall down on that (wobble off the string here), and end up being unkind and selfish. When that happens we have to put things right and get back to being kind and loving again. (Go back to walking along the string again.)

Have some pictures of people behaving well and badly. Show the pictures one by one, and decide together whether the people are walking God's way or not. If they are, put the picture on the string; if not, place it away from the string. Copy the pictures below or use your own ideas. They need to be pictures your particular group can relate to.

Praying

To the tune of *Here we go round the mulberry bush.* Act out the verses and add or alter them as appropriate for the group. The children's ideas can be incorporated too.

Help us, God, to share our toys,
share our toys, share our toys,
help us, God, to share our toys,
and live as Jesus told us.

Other verse ideas: to help our mums/help our dads; to look after our pets; to tell the truth.

Activities

On the worksheet there is a chart to be filled in through the week to draw attention to their good, brave and honest behaviour, and a 'spot the loving living' activity. They can also be taught Jesus' summary of the law using their fingers. They simply touch each finger of one hand (as if counting) as they say the words 'Love God, love each other'.

Notes

Love God, love each other

To do this week

Monday	Tuesday	Wednesday	Thursday	Friday	Saturday

Colour in a 'thumbs up' when you are

Good

Brave

Honest

For parents
You can sing this prayer to 'Here we go round the mulberry bush'.
You can make up other verses too.

Help us God, to share our toys,
share our toys, share our toys,
help us God, to share our toys,
and live as Jesus told us.

Other verse ideas:
to help our mums/help our dads
to look after our pets
to tell the truth.

Talk about the things you spot

Spot the loving living!

Second Sunday of Lent

Thought for the day

God's glory transfigures Jesus as he prays on the mountain. Our lives, too, can become increasingly radiant as the Spirit transforms us.

Readings

Genesis 15:5-12, 17-18
Psalm 26
Philippians 3:17-4:1
Luke 9:28-36

Aim

To look at how lives can shine with God's love.

Starter

Patches of sunshine. Have some cut-out circles of yellow paper scattered on the floor and explain that these are patches of sunshine in a dark wood. The children move and dance around to some music, and when the music stops they go and stand on a sunshine patch. Take away a patch each time so that in the end there is only one patch of sunshine left. Children not finding a patch to stand on are out.

Teaching

Talk about how much we need the sunshine. We need God's love to shine in the world too. God can help us to make our lives shine like patches of sunshine in the dark forest. Put out the sunshine patches again, and this time tell the children to stand in the darkness when you say something which is bad or sad, and go to a sunshine patch when you say something good and loving.

Bad and Sad
People hitting and hurting each other
Being grumpy and sulky
Being a pain
People not having anywhere to live
People telling lies
People not having enough to eat

Good and Loving
People saying sorry
Being friendly
Helping someone
People sharing their things with others
People telling the truth
People giving money to buy food for the starving

By physically moving into the sunshine when the 'shining lives' qualities are mentioned, the children will begin to understand the symbolism of radiant light in a spiritual sense. Jesus' life shone because of what he said and what he did. Our lives can shine with his love like patches of sunshine.

Praying

You will need the children to have made their sunshine mats for this. They start by standing on the mat and singing to the tune of *Twinkle, twinkle, little star.* At the darkness section the children move off the mat and walk around it, first one way and then the other, before moving back on to the mat for the last line.

We are sunshine in the darkness,
we are shining with your love.
Help us when we live in darkness,
help us when we live in darkness,
help all those who live in darkness
to shine like sunshine with your love!

Activities

Have some sheets of yellow paper with a wavy outline drawn on. Children old enough to use scissors can cut these out. Others will need help here. Or use white paper and let the children colour them with yellow crayons. The prayer from the sheet can be cut out and stuck on to the mat so that parents can sing the prayer with their children at home. The sheet also includes a drawing activity and a puzzle to see which behaviours belong to the 'light'.

Notes

Cross out the unloving things and colour the sunshine things in bright colours.

Parents: Cut out, stick on the sunshine mat, and sing the prayer together.

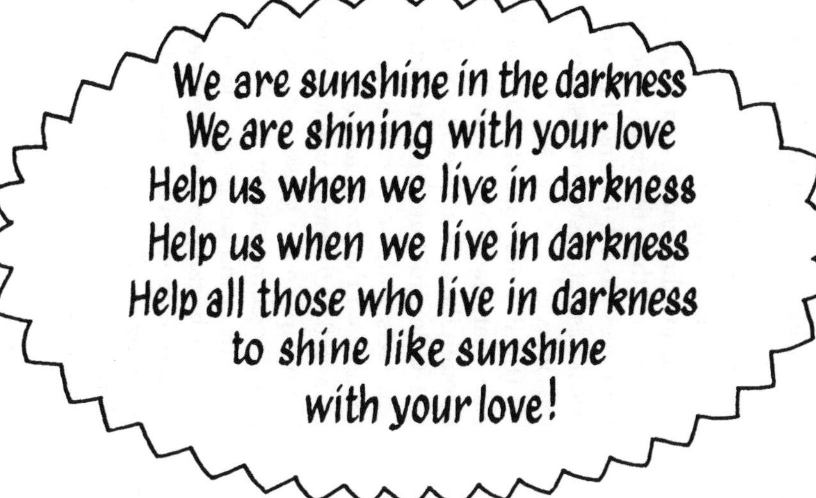

Draw something which makes you happy.

Draw something which makes you sad.

Third Sunday of Lent

Thought for the day

The great 'I AM' calls people in every generation to repent so that God's kingdom can be established and grow.

Readings

Exodus 3:1-8, 13-15
Psalm 102
1 Corinthians 10:1-6, 10-12
Luke 13:1-9

Aim

To understand that God wants to help us grow in love and goodness.

Starter

Have a selection of balls and bean bags, enough for each child to have one. Encourage them to practise their throwing and catching, so that they get better and better at it.

Teaching

Gather everyone in a circle and share with each other what you were all practising, and how you got on. Be encouraging and make certain that you are praising the way they have all been working hard at difficult things, rather than praising one 'expert'.

Following Jesus is something we can get better and better at as we practise, and we can all help one another along, encouraging each other in being loving and thoughtful, and trusting God.

Now tell them this story, which they listen to with their eyes closed. During the story quietly place a small vase of fresh flowers down in the middle of the circle.

This is a story about you. You are opening a big gate that leads into a secret garden. You walk through the gate and feel the soft grass under your feet. Colourful butterflies are flitting about, and the sun feels warm on your back. You can see your shadow on the grass, and a tiny ladybird climbing up a stalk. All around you are flowers – daisies and buttercups in the grass, red and yellow roses and blue forget-me-nots in the flower beds. There are apple trees and weeping willow trees. You can hear the bees buzzing and you feel happy in the garden.

You sit down on the grass and watch the gardener watering the flowers, snipping off dead bits of the plants and clearing the ground around them all in order to help them grow well. You see the gardener stop and look carefully at one plant which is looking rather a mess. You think to yourself that he might as well throw this plant away, as it hasn't grown any flowers or fruit for ages.

But the gardener is carefully looking after the plant. He's digging in some plant food around the roots, clearing away some strong weeds, and cutting the plant back a bit. Now he's giving it a good long drink, to make sure it has everything it needs to grow well. You think to yourself that the gardener must be very fond of all his plants to spend all that time on one which hasn't even been flowering. No wonder the garden feels a happy place to be. All the plants must know that the gardener loves and cares for them and will do everything he can to help them grow well.

You pick a few flowers and take them with you through the big gate and out of the garden. You take the flowers home and give them to someone you love. Then you suddenly find yourself back in the Treasure Seekers group at church, with the leaders and the other children, and there, in the middle of the circle, is a little bunch of flowers from that secret garden!

Praying

Dear Father God,
you are like a good gardener,
the way you look after us all
and love us
and help us to grow well.
Thank you! Amen.

Activities

On the sheet there is an outline of the garden, and the children can draw in the flowers and trees which the gardener loves and looks after, or they can stick on ready-cut shapes of coloured paper for flowers, with green wool stalks.

Notes

To pray with your child
Dear Father God,
you are like a
good gardener,
the way you look
after us all and
love us and help
us to grow well.
Thank you! Amen.

Fourth Sunday of Lent

Thought for the day

Be reconciled with God. He is waiting to welcome us.

Readings

Joshua 5:9-12
Psalm 33
2 Corinthians 5:17-21
Luke 15:1-3, 11-32

Aim

To know that God our Father is welcoming and forgiving.

Starter

Play a welcoming circle game. Everyone sits in a circle and the leader starts describing someone in the group. Everyone says together, 'I'd like to meet that person – who can it be?' The person concerned stands up and says, 'It's ME!' Everyone shakes hands with them or claps, before the leader describes someone else.

Teaching

Tell the children this story.

Yow Bear lived with a boy called David, who loved him very much. When David pedalled his car, Yow was always there sitting beside him, hanging out over the side and watching the pavement racing past underneath them. When David went to bed at night, Yow Bear snuggled in beside him. Sometimes he went exploring once David was asleep, but when that happened he couldn't quite manage to jump up on the bed again, so David would wake up to find Yow Bear lying on the floor.

If David was ever very cross or very sad, Yow Bear would either get stamped on a lot or cried on a lot, so he was quite a floppy bear and had been mended many times.

Yow Bear was a well-travelled Bear as David tucked him under his arm and took him with him everywhere he went. So Yow had been on a ferry (and hoped he wouldn't be dropped in the water), he'd been to school to see David's sister in a play, he'd been in buses and trains and cars.

One day there was jam tart and custard for pudding and David suddenly said, 'Can Yow Bear have . . . Where *is* Yow Bear?' And Yow Bear was lost. He wasn't under the bed or in the bath. He wasn't in any of the places he sometimes hid in. Everyone searched the whole flat, and nobody found him. Everyone was so sad that they didn't feel like eating the hot jam tart and custard.

Then Mum remembered where they had all walked that morning, watching a tractor at work, so she went outside to search for him there. David cried into Dad's sweater and hated the world.

After a while everyone heard the door open, and Mum's feet climbing the stairs to the flat. 'Growl, growl!' said Mum in Yow Bear's growly voice. David shot off Dad's lap and grabbed Yow very tight, hugging him and beaming away through his tears. Everyone was smiling and laughing and so happy that Yow Bear was home again. And everyone decided they'd like some jam tart and custard after all!

Praying

God our Father,
we belong to you and love you
and know that you love us.
Being with you makes us happy.
Amen.

Activities

The worksheet can be made into a 'welcome home' poster which they decorate with scrunched-up tissue paper, or an assortment of shiny and colourful scraps of paper, foil, and wool. The poster can then be hung up at home to welcome anyone who has been away.

Notes

Welcome home!
For parents to pray with your child
God our Father,
we belong to you
and love you
and know that
you love us.
Being with you
makes us happy.
Amen.

FIFTH SUNDAY OF LENT

Thought for the day

It is not God's wish to condemn anyone, but he longs for us to turn to him and live.

Readings

Isaiah 43:16-21
Psalm 125
Philippians 3:8-14
John 8:1-11

Aim

To see that God is in the sad and hard times as well as the happy ones.

Starter

Have an assortment of junk, crayons, paint, wool and glue. Tell the children that all this is stuff that no one wants. It's stuff that people have thrown out as rubbish. But we can use it to make things. Set the children free to transform the junk, and then share and admire what we all managed to make.

Teaching

Talk about the fun we've had with some old boxes and thrown-out rubbish. God never thinks of anything or anybody as rubbish. He can make beautiful things out of everything. Show some seed. What does God make out of this dried up, dusty stuff? Flowers! (Show some pictures from a seed catalogue.) Show some vegetable peelings and old tea bags. What can God do with this smelly old stuff? Compost to help the tomatoes grow! (Show some ripe compost.)

It's the same with people. God doesn't think, 'Oh, they're too small for me. I can't work with them.' He thinks, 'Ah, good! Some small people to cheer someone up, or give their mum a hug, or teach the grown-ups. Just what I needed!' And he doesn't think, 'Oh, they're no good to me now they're old and can't get out much.' He thinks, 'Ah, good! Some old people who can't get out much, so they've lots of time to think and pray for the holiday club. Just what I needed!' For God nothing is rubbish and nobody is rubbish.

God can even use the times we are sad. He can even use the bad things like accidents and wars, and make something good come from them. Nothing and nobody is too bad for God to use, because he loves us all.

Praying

Loving God,
I am glad you love us so much.
I am glad I can help you now
as well as when I am grown-up.
You can use my sadness as well as my happy times
whenever you like. Amen.

Activities

If the children need more time to finish their junk models they can do that now. The worksheet helps them think about the good that God can bring out of such things as moving house, a rainy holiday, and a time in hospital. Make sure they understand that God never makes bad things happen to us, but when they do happen he always works to use them for some good.

Notes

How can God bring good out of this?

My junk model looks like this

For parents
Pray with your child each night as you kiss them goodnight.

Loving God,
I am glad you love us
so much.
I am glad I can help you
now as well as when I am
grown up. You can use my
sadness as well as my happy
times whenever you like.
Amen.

Jesus liked making things too

Palm (Passion) Sunday

Thought for the day

As Jesus rides into Jerusalem on a donkey, and the crowds welcome him, we sense both the joy at the Messiah being acclaimed, and the heaviness of his suffering which follows. Jesus' mission is drawing to its fulfilment.

Readings

Liturgy of the Palms:
Luke 19:28-40

Liturgy of the Passion:
Isaiah 50:4-7
Psalm 21
Philippians 2:6-11
Luke 22:14-23:56 or Luke 23:1-49

Aim

To introduce them to the story of the entry into Jerusalem.

Starter

Stop, wave, shout hooray! When different signs are displayed the children 'Stop!' (a red circle), 'Wave!' (a cut-out or real palm branch), and 'Shout hooray!' (a crown). You can also sing a praise song, such as *Sing Hosanna*.

Teaching

Using upturned bowls and pots and a green cloth or large towel, let the children help make a model landscape. Boxes covered in white paper make the Jerusalem buildings, and the path down into the Kidron valley is a length of brown crêpe paper or material. Cut out coat shapes of fabric which the children can lay down on the road in front of Jesus, and have a card cut-out of Jesus riding on the donkey which you can move along as you tell the story. Let the children all wave their paper palm branches, standing around the model. They will feel as if they are all part of the story.

Praying

Hooray for Jesus,
riding on a donkey!
Hooray for Jesus,
he is our King!
Hooray for Jesus,
coming to Jerusalem!
Hooray for Jesus,
he is our King!

Activities

Today the children may be joining in the parish procession, with streamer-waving, singing and dancing. They will also be preparing the model. Have large palm leaves drawn on green sugar paper. Older children can cut these out themselves, and those just mastering the scissors technique can make random cuts along the sides of the basic shape. Pictures to help with this and the houses are given on the worksheet. There is also a picture of the event which the children can complete by drawing in the people cheering Jesus on his way.

Notes

Palm branches

green paper

cut out

Houses

boxes

white paper

draw the window and door and stairs

For parents

Pray this together when you can shake or jangle keys, or dried peas in a jar.

Hooray for Jesus riding on a donkey!
Hooray for Jesus he is our king!
Hooray for Jesus coming to Jerusalem!
Hooray for Jesus he is our king!

Can you help finish the picture?
Draw in the missing bits.
Draw in lots of people, cheering Jesus on.

HOSANNA!

EASTER

Easter Day

If possible, it is recommended that the children and young people are in church with the other age groups today. Use and adapt some of the all-age ideas from the *Living Water* Complete Resource Book, and involve the children in some of the music and in the decorating of the church.

Thought for the day

It is true. Jesus is alive for all time. The Lord of life cannot be held by death. God's victory over sin and death means that new life for us is a reality.

Readings

Acts 10:34, 37-43
Psalm 117
Colossians 3:1-4
John 20:1-9

Aim

To enjoy celebrating that Jesus is alive.

Starter

Have an Easter egg hunt, preferably outside if this is safe and practical.

Teaching

Palm Tree publish a version of the Resurrection story called *Jesus is risen;* or you could tell the story gathered around an Easter garden that the children have helped to make.

Praying

Jesus died for us

(arms out, head down)

Now he's alive for us

(jump up and clap hands over head)

Hip, hip, HOORAY!

Jesus is alive today!

(raise arms)

Activities

Use plasticine or playdough for the children to make their own models of the garden, and the women coming to the empty tomb. On the worksheet there is a picture of the women visiting the tomb early on the first Easter morning.

Notes

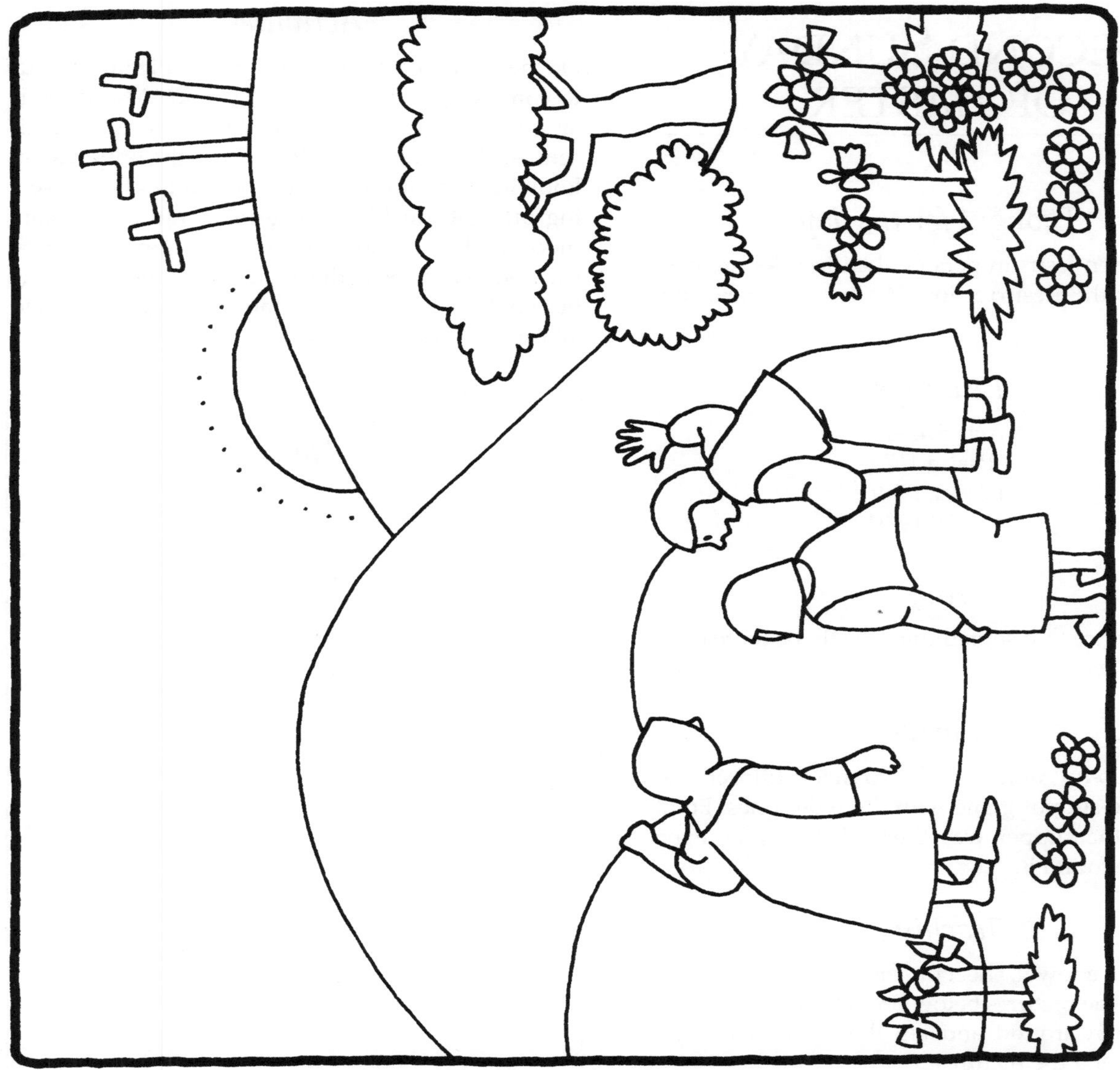

JESUS IS ALIVE!

Where are the Easter *eggs*?

Can you find 10 *eggs*?

For parents

Pray with your child, using the actions.

Jesus died for us (arms out, head down)
Now he's alive for us (jump up and clap hands over head)
Hip, hip, HOORAY!
Jesus is alive today (raise arms)

Second Sunday of Easter

Thought for the day

Having seen Jesus in person, the disciples are convinced of the Resurrection. We too can meet him personally.

Readings

Acts 5:42-47
Psalm 117
1 Peter 1:3-9
John 20:19-31

Aim

To experience that something can still be there even if we can't see it.

Starter

Play a peep-bo game with the younger children and a hunt-the-slipper game with the older ones. Point out that the slipper was there all the time, even before we found it.

Teaching

Spread out a towel, sheet or carpet tiles on the floor and copy the pictures below on to thin card. Gather the children around and tell the story of today's Gospel, using the pictures.

Praying

Dear Jesus,
I can't see you
but I know you are here.
I know you can hear me,
and I know you love me.
Thank you, Jesus! Amen.

Activities

On the worksheet there is a dot-to-dot picture of Jesus to complete, and a picture to colour. Also there is an activity which helps the children appreciate their senses, and realise that sight is not the only way of knowing something is true. Possibilities for the seeing but not touching category would be the sun, moon and stars; hearing but not seeing might be someone's heartbeat, the wind, or thunder; touching but not hearing might be a table or a sandwich; and all three might be a person.

Notes

Join the dots to make Jesus appear.

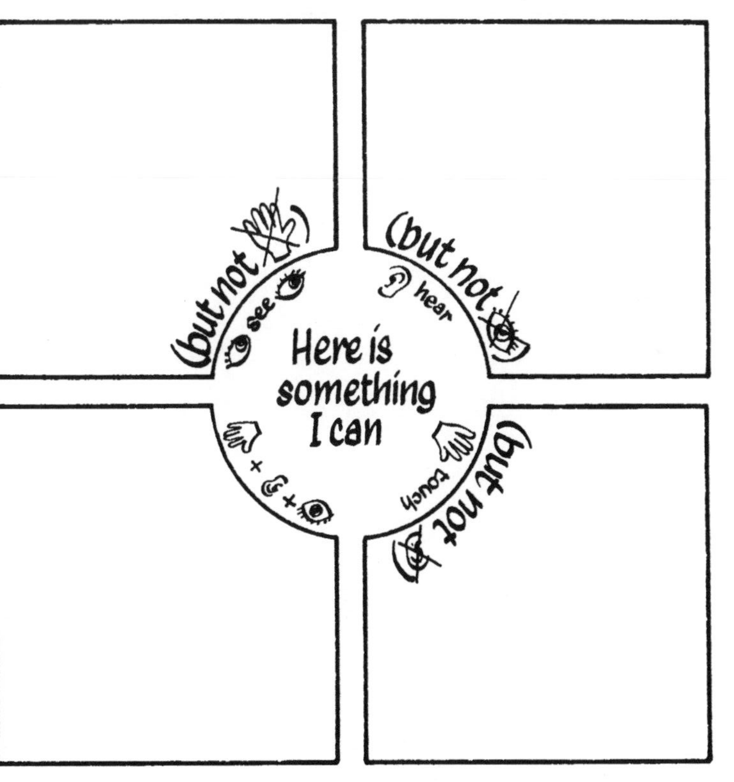

For parents
To pray with your child

Dear Jesus,
I can't see you
but I know you are here.
I know you can hear me,
and I know you love me.
Thank you, Jesus! Amen.

Third Sunday of Easter

Thought for the day

Those who know Jesus and recognise that he is the anointed Saviour are commissioned to go out as his witnesses to proclaim the good news.

Readings

Acts 5:27-32, 40-41
Psalm 29
Apocalypse 5:11-14
John 21:1-19

Aim

To get to know the story of today's Gospel.

Starter

Going fishing. Borrow or make the kind of magnet rod and lines which can catch paper fish with paperclips on their mouths. Have the paper fish cut ready so the children can decorate them and add the paperclips. Put the fish in a carton pond, and let fishing commence!

Teaching

Tell the story with the children all acting. They push the boat into the water, throw the net out into the water, wait, inspect the net, wait some more, and get fed up. Then catch sight of a man on the beach, cup your hand to your ear to hear what he says, pull in the net, throw it in the other side and haul in the massive catch. Realise that the man on the beach is Jesus, give a great shout, wade to shore and enjoy breakfast together.

Praying

Dear Jesus,
thank you for coming with us
to the shops / on the bus / to the dentist.
Wherever we go
you are always there for us. Amen.

Activities

If you get enough small cartons, each child can colour one to make a complete fishing set to take home. The worksheet has the outline for a collage picture which can be completed by sticking on cotton wool clouds, shiny paper fish and a red shiny paper fire on the beach. There is also a fish jigsaw with the words 'It's Jesus!' on it.

Notes

Stick on the fish, clouds sunshine and fire.

'Come and have breakfast!' shouted Jesus.

Colour the fish

Cut it out
cut it up.
Do the jigsaw!

For parents
You can adapt this prayer to use wherever you are going, and say it together on the way.

Dear Jesus,
Thank you for coming with us to the shops/on the bus/to the dentist.
Wherever we go you are always there for us.
Amen.

Fourth Sunday of Easter

Thought for the day

Jesus, the Good Shepherd, leads his flock into eternal life.

Readings

Acts 13:14, 43-52
Psalm 99
Apocalypse 7:9, 14-17
John 10:27-30

Aim

To know that Jesus is like a shepherd to us and we are like his sheep and lambs.

Starter

Lay on the floor a blue sheet to be water and some green paper clumps of grass. The children crawl around being sheep and lambs, and one child is dressed up (in nativity play costume or dressing-gown and tea-towel) as a shepherd who leads them around the room, taking them to the water for a drink, and the grass to graze.

Teaching

Show the children some pictures (from books or calendars) of shepherds with their sheep, and talk about the way the shepherd is there to look after the sheep and lambs, and take them safely to green pastures and fresh streams of water.

Now show them a picture (from a children's Bible) of Jesus with some children. Jesus is like a shepherd to us and we are like his sheep and lambs. All through every day of our whole life, Jesus leads us safely, and one day, when we die, he will lead us safely into heaven.

Praying

Loving Shepherd, lead me
through each day of my life.
Lead me safely to heaven.
Amen.

Activities

The sheet can be made into a mobile of sheep with their shepherd. Each child will also need cotton wool or chopped white knitting wool to stick on the sheep, wool or string to hang the sheep and shepherd and prayer, and a metal coat hanger.

Notes

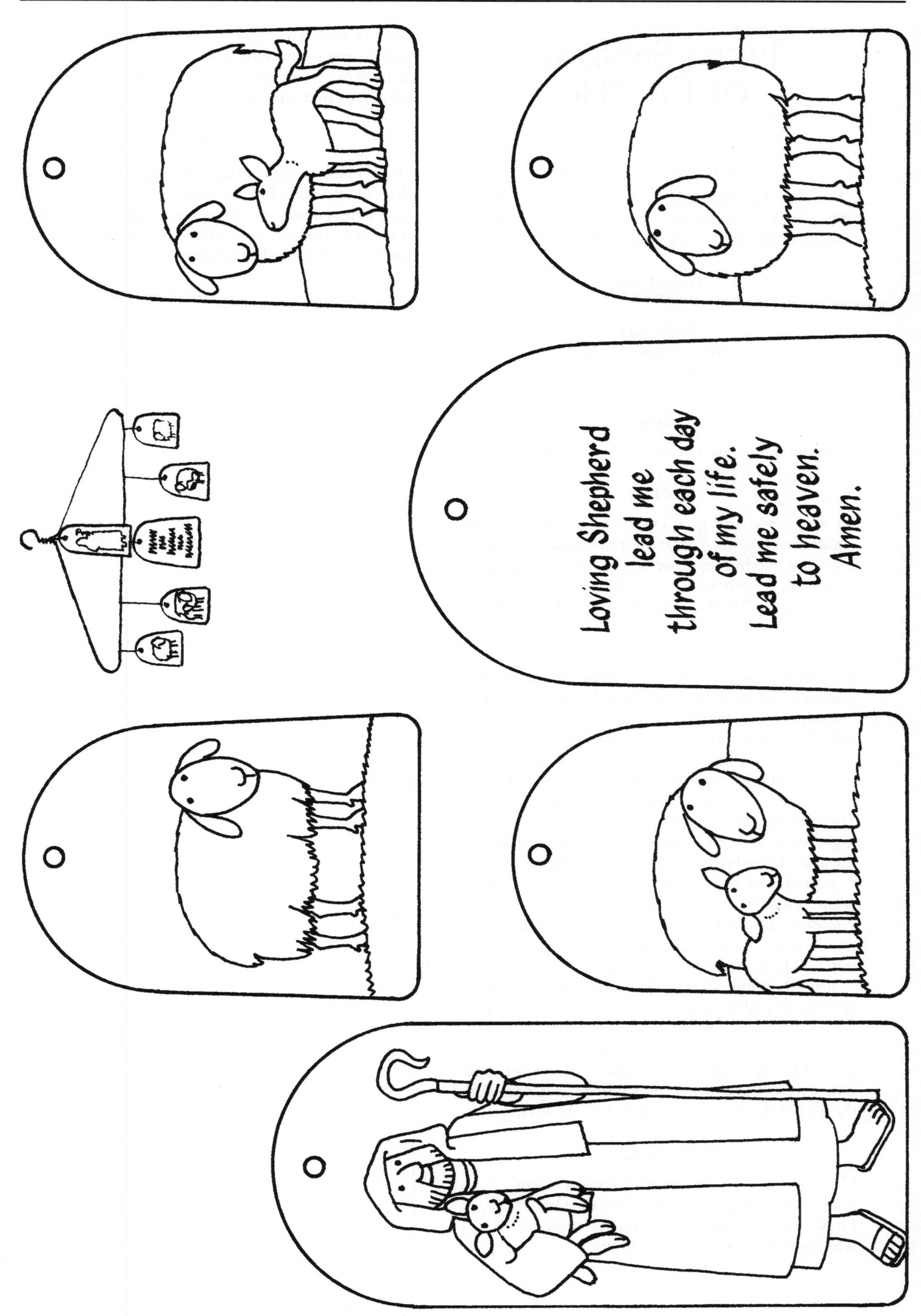
Loving Shepherd
lead me
through each day
of my life.
Lead me safely
to heaven.
Amen.

Fifth Sunday of Easter

Thought for the day

Christ, breaking through the barrier of sin and death, allows us to break into an entirely new way of living which continues into eternity.

Readings

Acts 14:21-27
Psalm 144
Apocalypse 21:1-5
John 13:31-35

Aim

To know that Jesus' friends love one another.

Starter

Sit in a circle and give everyone a chance to talk about their friends – what their names are and what they like playing together. Then play a circle game as friends together, such as 'The princess slept for 100 years', or 'In and out of the dusky bluebells'.

Teaching

Explain that today we are thinking about friends, and we're going to find out about Jesus and some of *his* friends. The children can do all the actions as you talk about the way Jesus and his friends went for walks together, listened to each other (cup hand to ear), talked together (open and close hands to make them 'chat'), laughed together and cried together. They sometimes went to parties and ate nice food together and drank refreshing drinks together. At the end of the day they got tired together (yawn).

Jesus loved his friends and he said to them, 'I want you to love one another like this. Even when you don't feel like it, I want you to be kind to one another and look after one another.' And that's what all Jesus' friends try and do.

Jesus has lots of friends. There are the friends who lived with him in Galilee, and there's all of us who follow Jesus today. We can be his friends as well – when we walk together, listen to each other, talk together, laugh together and cry together. And when we eat and drink, and when we get tired at the end of the day, Jesus is still with us, loving us.

Praying

I have a friend who is deeper than the ocean,
I have a friend who is wider than the sky,
I have a friend who always understands me,
whether I'm happy or ready to cry.

Jesus is my friend who is deeper than the ocean,
Jesus is my friend who is wider than the sky,
Jesus is my friend who always understands me,
whether I'm happy or ready to cry.

Activities

The worksheet has pictures to encourage the children to explore what it means to live in the loving way which marks us out as Jesus' friends, and they can fold, cut out and colour a string of Jesus' friends who are holding hands.

Notes

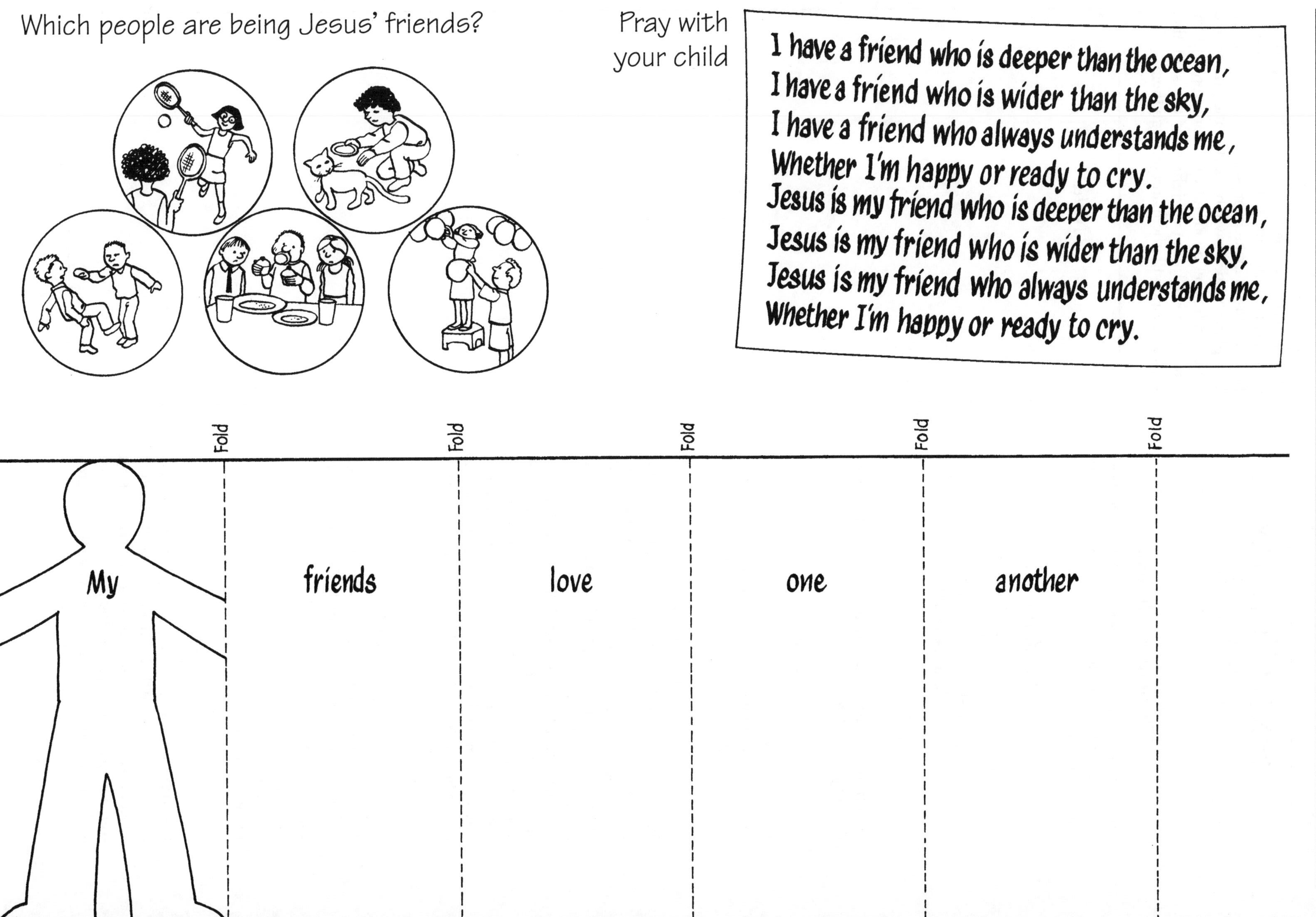
Which people are being Jesus' friends?
Pray with your child
I have a friend who is deeper than the ocean,
I have a friend who is wider than the sky,
I have a friend who always understands me,
Whether I'm happy or ready to cry.
Jesus is my friend who is deeper than the ocean,
Jesus is my friend who is wider than the sky,
Jesus is my friend who always understands me,
Whether I'm happy or ready to cry.
Fold
Fold
Fold
Fold
Fold
My
friends
love
one
another

Sixth Sunday of Easter

Thought for the day

The continuing presence of God, as Holy Spirit, leads us, as Jesus promised, into a personally guided outreach to all nations.

Readings

Acts 15:1-2, 22-29
Psalm 66
Apocalypse 21:10-14, 22-23
John 14:23-29

Aim

To introduce them to the idea of going where God the Holy Spirit leads us.

Starter

Follow my leader. Choose several children to take turns at leading everyone around to music, walking, hopping or dancing in the way they choose.

Teaching

Talk together about when we say goodbye, and practise waving to one another and blowing kisses. Talk about feeling sad when the time comes for saying goodbye to friends or grandparents and we don't want them to go.

Explain how Jesus' friends didn't want him to go, and when the time came to say goodbye they were sad. They didn't look forward to being without him. Jesus wanted them to know that he would not be leaving them on their own. The Holy Spirit of God would be coming to be with them and lead them in the right direction.

Praying

As you lead the children through a drawn or marked pathway, lead them also line by line in this prayer:

Spirit of God,
lead me along the paths
of kindness
and love. Amen.

Activities

The idea of leading is continued in the worksheet where they can take their finger for a walk through the country. There is also a matching activity to start you talking about keeping in touch with God so that we know where we are being led. Give the children the opportunity to ask for God's help and guidance in any areas of their life which they are a bit scared about, or which make them sad. Their recording of these places visually will be part of the prayer, and you can talk later about how God answered them. Children need to know right from the start that God can work with them and through them.

Notes

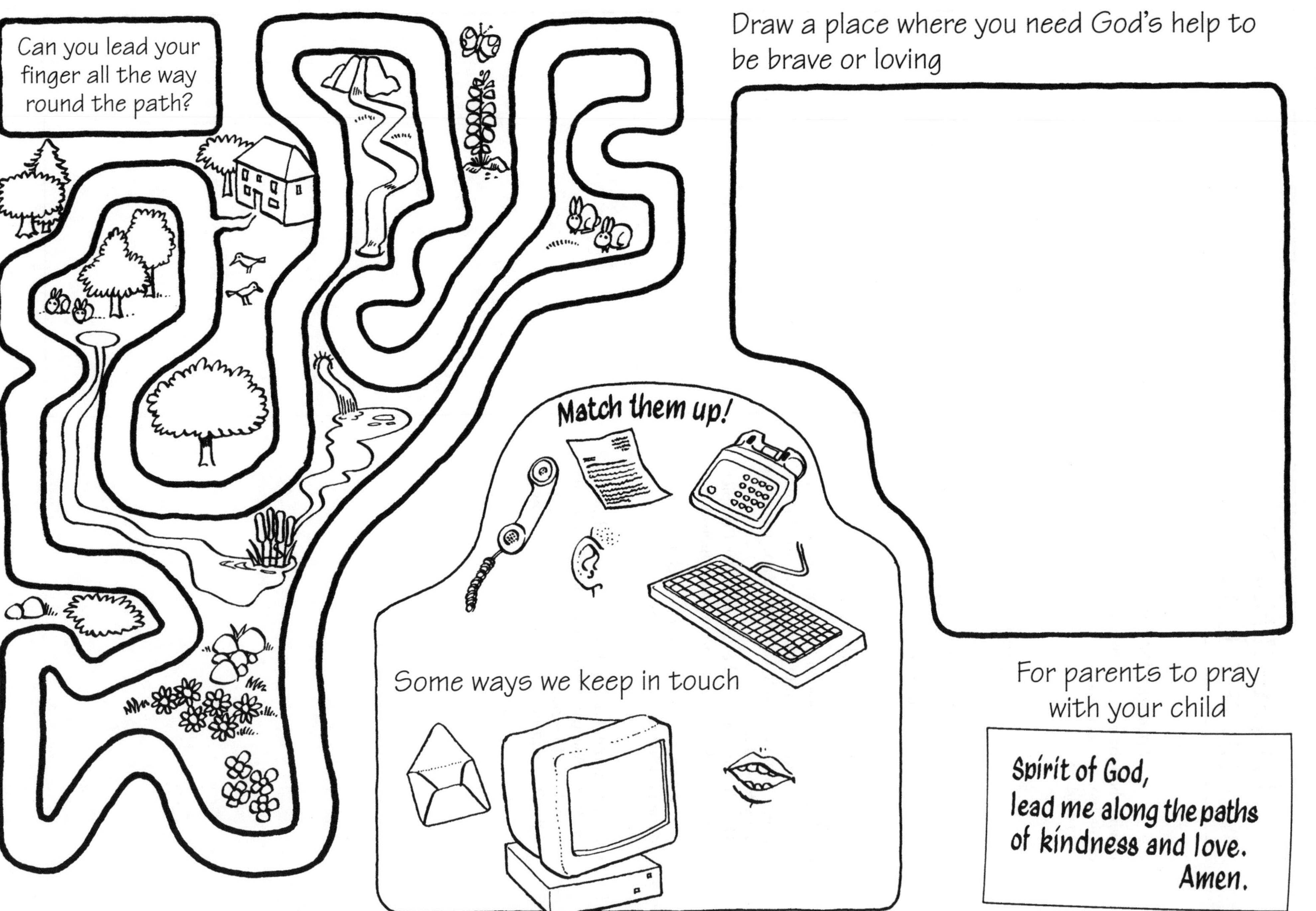
Can you lead your
finger all the way
round the path?
Draw a place where you need God's help to
be brave or loving
Match them up!
Some ways we keep in touch
For parents to pray
with your child
Spirit of God,
lead me along the paths
of kindness and love.
Amen.

THE ASCENSION OF THE LORD

Thought for the day

Having bought back our freedom with the giving of his life, Jesus enters into the full glory to which he is entitled.

Readings

Acts 1:1-11
Psalm 46
Ephesians 1:17-23
Luke 24:46-53

Activities

It is likely that Ascension Day services for schools will not need a separate programme for children. However, I have included a drawing and colouring activity for today.

The all-age ideas in the *Living Water* Complete Resource Book include the following suggestions.

- Any artwork or writing that the children have done on what the Ascension is about can be displayed around the building.
- Have a beautiful helium balloon at the ready. Write on it an Ascension message that the children would like to send. After the service two representative children can let the balloon float away.

Notes

Seventh Sunday of Easter

Thought for the day

Jesus lives for all time in glory; we can live the fullness of Resurrection life straight away.

Readings

Acts 7:55-60
Psalm 96
Apocalypse 22:12-14, 16-17, 20
John 17:20-26

Aim

For them to know that Jesus is in heaven, and explore what heaven is like.

Starter

Sit in a circle and describe different children and objects by giving clues about them. The children have to guess who or what is being described. (I'm thinking of something that is warm . . . and colourful . . . and has a hole to put your head through. What could it be?)

Teaching

Young children may not have been involved in Ascension Day services so tell them today about the friends of Jesus getting used to seeing him alive after Easter. Now the time has come for Jesus to go into heaven, and his friends won't see him any more. Use pictures cut out of card and move them around on carpet tiles or towels on the floor, with the children gathered round the outside of the landscape. Pictures to copy are given below. Cut out a large cloud to hide Jesus from their sight, and then take the friends back to Jerusalem rejoicing, before you add in the angels welcoming Jesus into heaven.

Praying

The angels said,
'Hallo, Jesus. Well done!'
I want to say it too:
'Hallo, Jesus.
Well done!'
Amen.

Activities

On the worksheet is a pattern for making angels. For the very young these will need to have been already copied and cut out. If you want to have lots of angels for each child use the template and cut the angels from that, perhaps using different colours of paper. Cotton or wool can be attached to the heads either by tying, or with sticky tape. Use shoe boxes for the surroundings of heaven, and white paper with cotton wool on it for the cloud. Use the picture of Jesus from the Ascension Day worksheet.

Notes

Colour your angel and cut it out. Put wool through the hole. Join (a) to (b)
cut
cut
Glue
Glue on back
a
b
Welcome, Jesus!
You can make lots of angels!
Jesus goes up to heaven
Draw the person who wears the crown
For parents
Pray with your child beside the model.
The angels said,
'Hallo, Jesus, Well done!'
I want to say it too:
'Hallo, Jesus. Well done!'
Amen.
Draw the person who wears this badge
5 metres
swimming

Pentecost

Thought for the day

As Jesus promised, the Holy Spirit is poured out on the apostles and the Church is born.

Readings

Acts 2:1-11
Psalm 103
1 Corinthians 12:3-7, 12-13
John 20:19-23

Aim

To celebrate the birthday of the Church.

Starter

Jack in the box. Have everyone crouching down. The leader says, 'Ready, steady, Jack in the box!', and everyone springs up. Vary the length of time between the 'ready' and the 'steady' so the children are hanging on the leader's words, ready to spring into action, but not sure when to.

Teaching

Explain how Jesus' friends had been told to wait for the coming of the Holy Spirit after Jesus had gone into heaven. They were praying and waiting, and waiting and praying for over a week, and then suddenly the Spirit came to them all.

Bring in a birthday cake with two candles on it. If possible, have the cake in the shape of a church, or have a picture or model of a church on it. Explain to the children that today is like the birthday of the Church, not just of St Andrew's but all the churches everywhere in the world. Light the candles, each of which stands for about a thousand years. It is now about two thousand years since the Holy Spirit of God was poured out on Jesus' friends and the Christian Church was born.

As you talk about the handing-on of the Gospel, use a set of Russian dolls, and keep taking another one out. Those few people told lots of others about Jesus, and those others told lots more, and their children and their grandchildren, and then the grandchildren grew up and they told their friends and their children and their grandchildren. And soon more and more people all over the world knew about Jesus and the love God has for us. And they went on telling other people until eventually someone told us! So now we know about Jesus and God's love for us, and through our lives we'll tell our friends and our children and our grandchildren so they will know as well.

Sing 'Happy Birthday, dear Church', blow out the candles and share the cake.

Praying

Happy birthday, dear Church,
Happy birthday, dear Church.
Jesus' love is for ever,
Happy birthday, dear Church!

Activities

Have some fairy cakes already iced, and let the children decorate them ready to give out to everyone as birthday cake after the service. The worksheet has a picture to colour of the Church being born at Pentecost.

Notes

FEASTS OF THE LORD

TRINITY SUNDAY

Thought for the day

The unique nature of God is celebrated today, as we reflect on the truth that God is Creator, Redeemer and Life-giver.

Readings

Proverbs 8:22-31
Psalm 8
Romans 5:1-5
John 16:12-15

Aim

To help them appreciate the wonder of God.

Starter

Let them make something, such as a picture, from all kinds of bits and pieces, such as wool, bottle tops, toffee wrappers and feathers. Or they can paint or print a picture. This activity needs to be fairly unstructured, so they express themselves in their pictures.

Teaching

Display all the pictures and admire them. Talk about how when we enjoy thinking of things and making them, we are doing what our God loves doing. He loves making things that are beautiful and huge and tiny. He loves making people, and watching over us as we grow and learn to do all sorts of things for ourselves, using the brain he has given us.

Pass round a few things God has made for the children to look at, touch and smell. Talk together about how lovely they are. (You might have a stone, a shell, a feather and a flower.)

Praying

Lord God,
I love the things you have made.
They show me your love. Amen.

Activities

Give the children large letters to colour and stick these with their pictures on to a long roll of wallpaper which can be displayed in church. The finished message reads: 'Our God is wonderful!' The worksheet also has this message, together with a dot-to-dot which again puts them in the role of creator so they can appreciate God as Creator.

Notes

Our God is wonderful

Have you ever
seen these?

To pray with your child

Lord God,
I love the things
you have made.
They show me
your love.
Amen.

Corpus Christi

Thought for the day

Jesus is the Living Bread, who brings us eternal life through Communion with him.

Readings

Genesis 14:18-20
Psalm 109
1 Corinthians 11:23-26
Luke 9:11-17

Activities

It is likely that Corpus Christi services for schools will not need a separate programme for children. However, I have included a worksheet for children in church today.

Notes

HONEY

How do you
like to eat bread?

Bread is good for us

Jesus says,

I am
the bread
of life

ORDINARY TIME

SECOND SUNDAY OF THE YEAR

Thought for the day

As a marriage celebrates the beginning of a changed, new life for the bride and groom, so our loving, faithful God has chosen us and is ready to transform our lives for the good of the world.

Readings

Isaiah 62:1-5
Psalm 95
1 Corinthians 12:4-11
John 2:1-12

Aim

To be introduced to the story of the wedding at Cana.

Starter

Water play. Protect the floor and have a number of washing-up bowls with water, containers and sieves. Let the younger children enjoy filling and emptying. Older children can be encouraged to see how many small containers it takes to fill a larger one.

Teaching

Talk with the children about any weddings they may have been to and taken part in. Show a few wedding photos (preferably amateur ones which show people enjoying themselves rather than in set poses). Now tell them about the time Jesus and his mother were invited to a wedding. When you get to the part about the water jars, fill a large jug with water. Pour some into a wine glass as you tell them about the servants pouring it out. The fact that it is of course still water can lead on to what happened in Cana. I think this is far preferable to the red colouring stunts which only turn it all into a magic trick.

Praying

Thank you for the falling rain.
(wiggle fingers downwards)
Thank you for the rising sap.
(draw fingers upwards over body, as if a tree)
Thank you for the juicy fruit.
(hold arms out with fingers hanging down)
Thank you for my favourite fruity drink! Amen.
(pretend to drink it)

Activities

On the worksheet they will be changing things and making them special, and this forms a basis for thinking about how God works in our lives. Instructions for making a clay or plasticine water pot are given on the sheet.

Notes

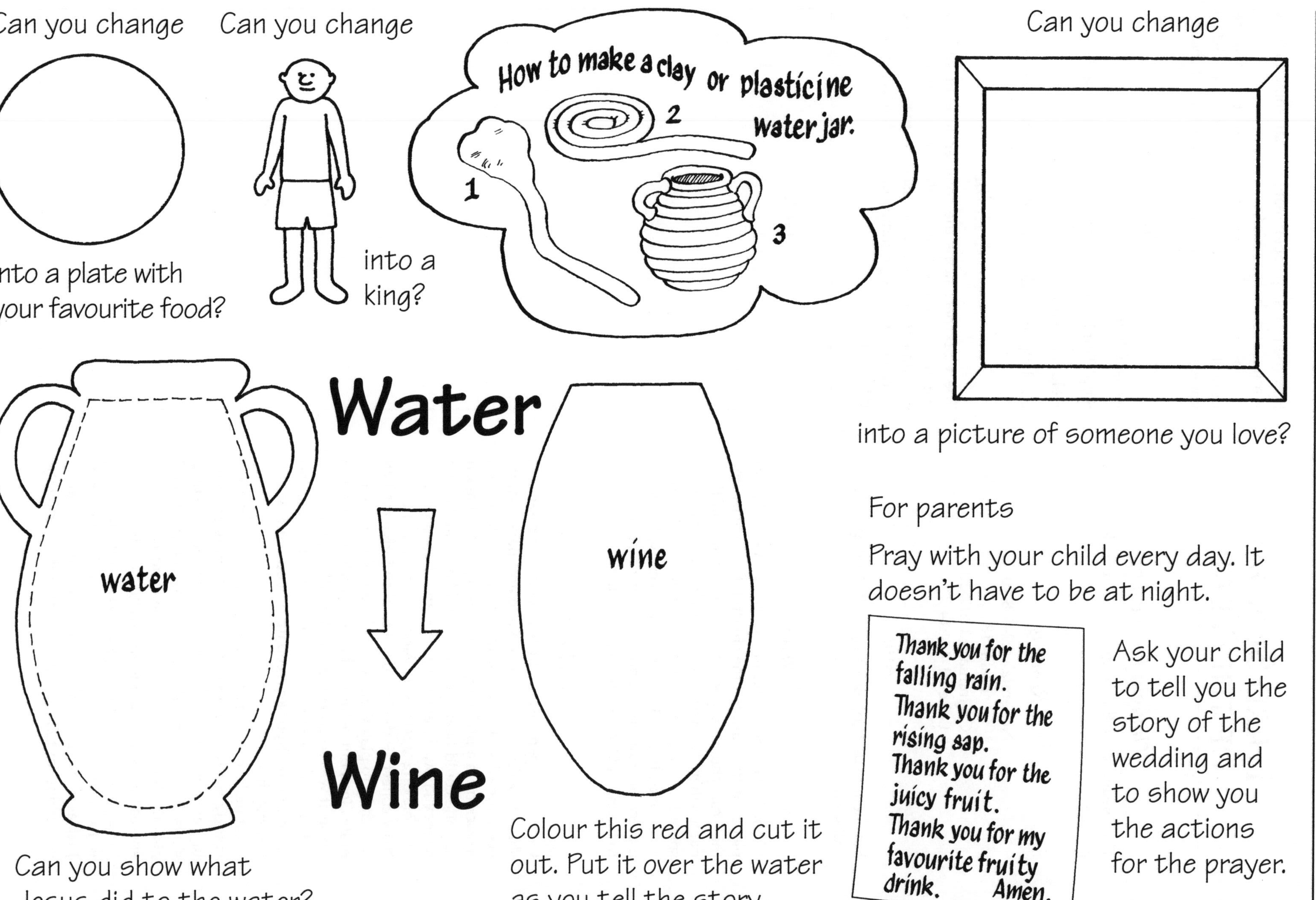
Can you change
into a plate with
your favourite food?
Can you change
into a
king?
How to make a clay or plasticine
water jar.
1
2
3
Can you change
into a picture of someone you love?
Water
Wine
water
wine
Can you show what
Jesus did to the water?
Colour this red and cut it
out. Put it over the water
as you tell the story.
For parents
Pray with your child every day. It
doesn't have to be at night.
Thank you for the
falling rain.
Thank you for the
rising sap.
Thank you for the
juicy fruit.
Thank you for my
favourite fruity
drink. Amen.
Ask your child
to tell you the
story of the
wedding and
to show you
the actions
for the prayer.

THIRD SUNDAY OF THE YEAR

Thought for the day

The meaning of the scriptures is revealed to the people.

Readings

Nehemiah 8:2-6, 8-10
Psalm 18
1 Corinthians 12:12-30
Luke 1:1-4; 4:14-21

Aim

For them to develop listening skills, both physically and spiritually.

Starter

Listen for your name. Sit in a circle. Have a plate of pieces of fruit and tell the children that one by one they can choose a piece to eat. You will call their name when it's their turn. For each one you can say something like, 'Max, you can jump to choose a piece of fruit now. Imogen, you can crawl to choose a piece of fruit now.' Speaking our name alerts us to listen, and God knows us by name.

Teaching

Give out percussion instruments (home-made shakers will be fine) to everyone and have a quiet bell yourself. Get everyone to play loudly, along with a track from a praise tape. Stop everyone and ask if anyone could hear the little bell. Play it on its own so they know what to listen for and then get everyone playing again, but listening out for the bell. Now collect all the instruments in and give the bell to a child to play while we all listen. Now it sounds quite clear, but before, when we were all making a noise, it was so quiet we could hardly hear it.

Stand at one end of the room facing the wall, and see if the children can creep up on you without you hearing them.

Sit in the circle again and try passing the bell (or a crackly, rustly bag) around the circle without it making any noise at all. All these things develop listening skills, both the attentiveness and concentration and also the body control. Praise the children for their success as some will find this quite a challenge. Tell the children how God helps us to know if something is right or wrong, and show this using puppets. Just as a puppet is thinking aloud about stealing something, or telling a lie or being unkind, ring the little bell. The puppet realises that something is wrong, and changes his/her action.

Explain that God never forces us to make the right choice (that's for us to decide) but he does let us know what is right, to help us make the right choice.

Praying

Jesus, when you say

Stop! Think! Change! *(ring the bell three times)*

Help me to hear you *(hands on ears)*

and help me to do it. Amen. *(hands out, palms up)*

Activities

The worksheet helps the children to explore how we hear best, both physically and spiritually. The instruments can then be used to make a storm, starting very quiet, building up and then dying away into silence.

Notes

Look at this picture. Edward is trying to tell his mum some news. Why can't she hear him?

Draw them in a quiet place so Edward can tell his news and his mum can hear it.

What is God saying?

God lets us know what is right and what is wrong

(but we do need to listen!)

For parents

Help your child to play a listening game this week.

Here is a prayer to pray together.

Jesus, when you say,
STOP! THINK! CHANGE!
Help me to hear you
and help me to do it.
Amen.

Fourth Sunday of the Year

Thought for the day

As a prophet, Jesus' work is to proclaim the reign of God's love, not only to the Jewish people but to the whole world.

Readings

Jeremiah 1:4-5, 17-19
Psalm 70
1 Corinthians 12:31-13:13
Luke 4:21-30

Aim

To look at what love is.

Starter

Have an 'I love it' face at one end of the room, an 'I hate it' face at the other, and an 'I don't really mind' face in the middle. You call out all sorts of different things – various foods, colours and things to do – and in each case the children run to the face which they agree with.

Teaching

Prepare a large red heart-shaped piece of paper folded like this so that you can open it up.

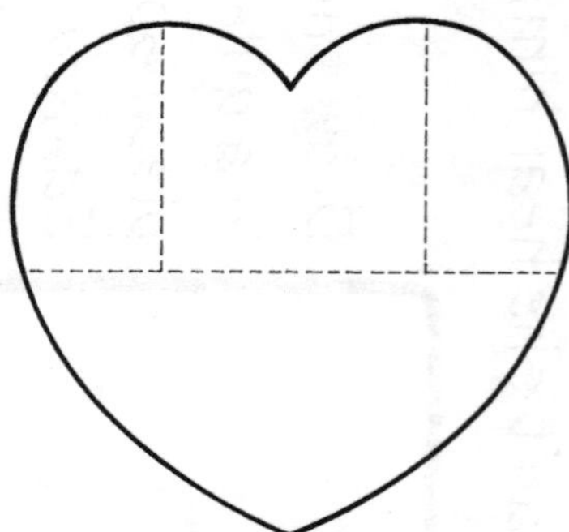

In our game there were some things we really loved, and some things we hated. In Treasure Seekers we are always saying that God loves us. We sing that God's love is so wide we can't get round it, so high we can't get over it and so low we can't get under it. (You might want to sing it now.) So what does that mean? What is God's wonderful love like? Here are some of the things the Bible tells us about love. (Open the heart and read the slips of paper which you have hidden inside:

- Love is kind.
- Love is never selfish.
- Love doesn't show off.
- Love cares for others.
- Love sees the good in people.
- Love is full of trust.
- Love goes on trying.
- Love doesn't get in a bad mood.
- Love lasts for ever.

That's how God loves each of us, and it makes God happy to see us loving one another like this as well.

Praying

Dear Father God
thank you for loving us.
Teach us to love one another.
Amen.

Activities

The children can do some loving act of kindness (like helping put the chairs away, or putting out the cups and biscuits for after Mass), and they can make the sheet into a sampler by threading coloured wool through the punched holes. (You may want to mount the sheets on thin card for extra strength. Punch inaccessible holes with a pencil, resting the sheet on Blu-Tack.)

Notes

DEAR FATHER GOD
THANK YOU
FOR LOVING US.
TEACH US
TO LOVE ONE ANOTHER
AMEN

Fifth Sunday of the Year

Thought for the day

God calls his people and commissions them.

Readings

Isaiah 6:1-8
Psalm 137
1 Corinthians 15:1-11
Luke 5:1-11

Aim

To introduce them to the story of the catch of fishes.

Starter

Have a fish-catching game, either using magnets on strings and paperclips on the fish, or a bazaar-stall fishing game with floating fish which are caught with hooks. The fish for the magnet game can either be made beforehand or cut out ready and then coloured by the children.

Teaching

Tell the story with the children acting it out as you go along. They can find their way to their boat in the dark, push their boat out, throw out the nets, sit and wait, pull in the nets and shake their heads when they find no fish, throw the nets out again, wait and yawn, pull the nets in, and repeat this until morning comes and they rub their eyes. They can shade their eyes to see all the crowds coming, beckon Jesus and help him into the boat, and sit on the sand to listen. Then they push the boat out again, throw in the nets, wait, and pull them in full of fish! Tell the children how Peter was amazed at what had happened, and a bit frightened by it. Jesus told him he didn't need to be afraid, and invited Peter to follow him. Peter said yes, and spent the rest of his life following Jesus and telling other people about him.

Praying

Sing this prayer to the tune of *One, two, three, four, five, once I caught a fish alive.*

One, two, three, four, five,
Thank you, God, that I'm alive!
Six, seven, eight, nine, ten,
Here I am to help you, then.
What job can I do?
Love God as he wants me to,
show his love each day
living life the loving way.

Activities

On the sheet the children create a collage picture of the story. You will need some scraps of net curtain or the net bags that oranges come in and some fish cut from shiny paper.

Notes

What a lot of fish!

To make the collage picture

1 Colour the picture
2 Stick on the fishing nets
3 Stick on lots and lots of fish

**One, two, three, four, five,
Thank you, God, that I'm alive!
Six, seven, eight, nine, ten,
Here I am to help you, then.
What job can I do?
Love God as he wants me to,
show his love each day,
living life the loving way.**

For parents

Please help your child learn this prayer by singing it together every day.

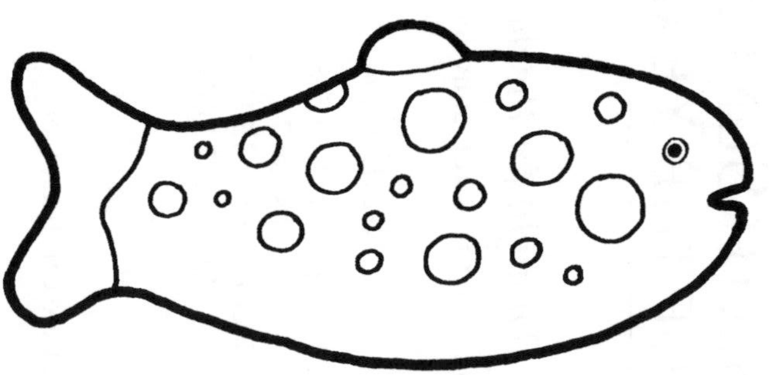

Cut out and colour this fish and put a paper clip at the mouth. Try catching it at home with a fridge magnet.

Sixth Sunday of the Year

Thought for the day

The challenges and rewards of living by faith.

Readings

Jeremiah 17:5-8
Psalm 1
1 Corinthians 15:12, 16-20
Luke 6:17, 20-26

Aim

To know that we can trust God.

Starter

Chickens. The children run and peck around until the mother hen clucks a danger warning. Whenever that happens, the chickens stop what they are doing and run to the safety of the mother hen (one of the leaders on a rug). When she tells them the danger is over, they can scatter again.

Teaching

Talk about how the chickens know they will be safe with the mother hen. They can trust her to look after them. Talk together about what happens if they fall over and hurt themselves, and draw their attention to the fact that because someone loves them, they look after them. Talk about the way they look after pets and the way they can look after their mums and dads and grandparents with hugs and helping them.

God looks after us all. He has given us a lovely world to live in, with food for us to eat, and all the things we need to make homes and clothes and toys and cars. That's because he loves us.

Praying

When I am afraid
I will trust in you, O God.
I will take shelter under your wings.

(From Psalms 56 and 57)

Activities

On the worksheet there are instructions for making a working model of chickens running to the safety of the mother hen's wings. You will need string and sticky tape, and may prefer to prepare the chicks and hen in card.

Notes

We can always trust Jesus
For parents
This prayer can be stuck on to the mother hen. Pray it with your child.
When I am afraid
I will trust in you, O God.
I will take shelter
under your wings.
Amen.
1 Colour and cut out
2 Make holes and thread strings.
Stick strings at back to card
3 When the mother hen clucks,
make the chicks run to her for safety

Seventh Sunday of the Year

Thought for the day

Jesus teaches us to love our enemies and forgive those who sin against us.

Readings

1 Samuel 26:2, 7-9, 12-13, 22-23
Psalm 102
1 Corinthians 15:45-49
Luke 6:27-38

Aim

To learn to make up when things go wrong.

Starter

Let the children draw on chalkboards and rub it all out again. Or use the magic writer pads that enable you to erase what you have drawn.

Teaching

Talk about and demonstrate how we can rub out our mistakes on a chalkboard. Draw a nasty splodge as you talk about someone being unkind. But then they say, 'I'm sorry I was unkind.' If someone says that to us we can say, 'That's OK. I forgive you!' As you say it, rub out the splodge.

Jesus says, 'Forgive one another. Pray for those who are unkind to you.' When we do this we are rubbing out the unkindness and clearing the way to start again.

Praying

Thank you, God,
for forgiving me.
Help me to forgive as well. Amen.

Activities

Help the children to make the two finger puppets from the worksheet and fix them on their fingers, so they can practise getting cross and making up again. They can also colour and fold the model on the sheet to see what a difference forgiveness makes.

Notes

Colour the finger puppets. Cut out and stick round fingers with rubber bands or sticky tape.

For parents

Ask your child to show you how to put things right when we are unkind and pray this prayer together.

Thank you, God
for forgiving me.
Help me
to forgive
as well.
Amen.

Colour the pictures. Cut out. Fold along the dotted lines. Now you can swing the middle flap over to make a 'before and after' story.

Grr!

Grr!

I'm sorry.
I forgive you!

I'm sorry.
I forgive you!

Eighth Sunday of the Year

Thought for the day

What we think important flows out in the way we speak.

Readings

Ecclesiasticus 27:4-7
Psalm 91
1 Corinthians 15:54-58
Luke 6:39-45

Aim

To know that God likes us to be our true selves with him.

Starter

Have some dressing-up clothes and masks so everyone can play at pretending to be someone or something else.

Teaching

Talk together about how we all dressed up and pretended to be clowns / rabbits / nurses / firemen. But all the time we knew who we really were. It's fun to play 'Let's pretend'. But there's another sort of pretending which isn't fun or good. It's when we have done something wrong, and we pretend we haven't done it at all. Like when Mum asks us if we've cleaned our teeth and we say yes, but we haven't. Or like when Dad asks if we left the bath taps on so the water overflowed, and we say it wasn't us, even though we really know it was. God wants us all to be honest and truthful. He wants us to be brave and say, 'Yes, it was me – and I'm sorry. What can I do to help put it right?' He wants us to know when we have been unkind, even if no one else knows it, so we can say in our prayers, 'Dear Father God, I know I got cross and grumpy today, and I'm sorry. Please help me get on with my brother / sister better tomorrow.'

God knows us already, really well. He knows when we think kind thoughts and when we think nasty, rude and unkind things. So with God we don't have to pretend. And God doesn't just know us really well – he loves us really well! And if we are always honest with God, God will be able to help us grow up into brave, honest and loving people.

Praying

Dear Father God,
you know all about me
and you love me as well.
Thank you for that! Amen.

Activities

On the sheet there is space to draw in white crayon or wax candle. Then provide thin watercolour for the children to paint over the sheet, and their lovely drawing will show through. If we stay close to Jesus, then Jesus' love will show in us right through our lives.

Notes

For parents to pray with your child

Dear Father God,
you know all
about me
and you love me
as well.
Thank you for that!
Amen.

Stay close to Jesus and his love will show through your life!

1. Draw a secret picture with wax.
2. Paint all over the square and your picture will show through

Ninth Sunday of the Year

Thought for the day

The good news we have been given is not just for us, but to pass on to the rest of the world.

Readings

1 Kings 8:41-43
Psalm 116
Galatians 1:1-2, 6-10
Luke 7:1-10

Aim

To learn how to start spreading the good news.

Starter

Sit in a circle and pass the parcel. Put a Christian sticker in each layer, and a Bible story book in the middle.

Teaching

Talk about the way they have been passing the parcel on, so everyone gets a turn, and how good they were at that. Now we're going to pass our news on to each other, but we don't need to put it in a parcel. We can speak our news and everyone will be able to hear it at once. Have a sharing news session, making sure the children listen to each other by passing a 'talking shell/stone' around. Only the one holding this can speak.

Tell the children that you have a piece of very good news you want to pass on to them. Holding the talking stone/shell tell them that you have found out that God is real and that he loves us all. Following Jesus makes you very happy and helps you live a good life. Ask if any of them know that piece of good news as well.

Tell the children that there are quite a lot of people who don't know this good news yet, and they need people to tell them. What can we do about that?

Write their ideas down. It doesn't matter that they can't read them; they know adults write things down that are important, and will pick up on the truth that their ideas are being taken seriously.

Praying

Lord Jesus,
I am sad that some people
don't know you yet.
Please bless them
and send someone
to tell them about you. Amen.

Activities

This will lead on from the ideas the children have. You may be scribing messages to go with their drawings that can be copied and given to Baptism families, or people being married in your church. You may be making posters to be put up where the slimming and line-dancing classes are held. You may be taping their messages. Have an assortment of materials at the ready.

The worksheet has a 'message delivery' activity, an outline to use for messages, and a 'matching people with message' puzzle.

Notes

Can you help the postman *give out* all the letters?
1
2
3
4
5
Messages
To pray with your child
Lord Jesus,
I am sad that some people
don't know you yet.
Please bless them and
send someone to tell
them about you.
Amen.
5
4
1
2
3
His leg is broken
Tickets, please
The fire is now out. Time for a cup of tea
Who is saying what?

TENTH SUNDAY OF THE YEAR

Thought for the day

Our God is full of compassion; he hears our crying and it is his nature to rescue us.

Readings

1 Kings 17:17-24
Psalm 29
Galatians 1:11-19
Luke 7:11-17

Aim

To get to know the story of the widow at Nain.

Starter

Sad and happy. Make a smiley face for one end of the room and a sad face for the other end. The children find a space in the middle. The leader calls out situations, and if it's something that makes them sad they run to the sad face; if happy, to the happy face. Situations may be eating chocolate, playing with friends, your pet being ill, going on holiday, having a tummy ache, and getting an invitation to a party.

Teaching

Bring the wall labels down and lay them on the floor together, back to back. Today we are going to hear about someone who started off being very sad (show this side) and Jesus helped to make her very happy (show the happy side.)

Tell the story, making sure the children understand what a widow is (otherwise they may assume you are talking about a window). When you tell them about her son dying, ask them how the mother was feeling, and show the sad face. How did Jesus know she was so sad? Let them add these details to the story. Take your time over telling them how Jesus raised the young man to life, pausing for a moment after he has said, 'Young man, get up'. When Jesus gives the young man back to his mother, look at the sad face again. Did the mother feel sad now? Change the face to match her joy.

Praying

Lord Jesus,
we pray for people who are sad.
Please help them to be happy again. Amen.

Activities

Make masks using paper plates with the eyes already cut out. They draw a happy face on one side and a sad one on the other.

Notes

Which things would make Jesus happy?
Which things would make Jesus sad?

God loves us!

To pray with your child

Lord Jesus,
We pray for people
who are sad.
Please help them to
be happy again.
Amen.

ELEVENTH SUNDAY OF THE YEAR

Thought for the day

God has the authority and the desire to forgive our sins completely and set us free from guilt.

Readings

2 Samuel 12:7-10, 13
Psalm 31
Galatians 2:16, 19-21
Luke 7:36-8:3

Aim

To know that God loves us and forgives us.

Starter

Have a number of sorting-out games, such as getting different shapes into the right holes, sorting out a Happy Families set of cards into families, and tidying a muddle of a cupboard or dressing-up box.

Teaching

Talk about what a good job we did of sorting those things out and putting things right again. Whenever we do that we're being like God, because God loves putting things right and sorting out the messes we make in our lives. Let's look at the sort of things God puts right.

Using toys or puppets, have them acting out various situations where someone is behaving wrongly. For instance, one toy can be greedy and take all the cakes, so there aren't enough for the others; there may be two being nasty to a third, and leaving them out all the time; 'Mum' may leave the children playing, and one keeps kicking or saying nasty things to the other. Vary the situations to suit your group. At the end of each situation let the children say what the wrong behaviour was, and think how they should have behaved. (This may be fun to find out!)

Talk about how we all behave badly sometimes, and the good thing is that, as soon as we realise we have done wrong, we can say 'I'm sorry' to God and 'I'm sorry' to the people we have upset. And then it can be put right straight away so we can get on with enjoying life again.

Praying

Thank you, Jesus,
for showing me
when I was being unkind.
I'm sorry I did it.
Thank you for forgiving me!

Activities

On the worksheet there are examples of unkind and selfish behaviour for the children to talk about, together with an activity to put right what is wrong. Even young children need to be taught about these things. It is important that the teaching is matched with friendly, trustworthy leaders and a secure, loving church environment. The children are invited to think of an area where they know they find it hard to behave well, and draw them doing it God's way. The process of drawing the right behaviour is positive reinforcement and will help develop good self-esteem.

Notes

What's wrong here?

Let's put it right!

Me, doing it *God's* way

To pray with your child.

**Thank you, Jesus,
for showing me when
I was being unkind.
I'm sorry I did it.
Thank you for
forgiving me!
Amen.**

Twelfth Sunday of the Year

Thought for the day

Following Christ means daily taking up our cross.

Readings

Zechariah 12:10-11
Psalm 62
Galatians 3:26-29
Luke 9:18-24

Aim

To help the children see that often things need to be broken before they can be used.

Starter

Break open a new pack of modelling clay while the children watch, and give them each a chunk to model with.

Teaching

You will need some cooking chocolate, shredded wheat, bowls and spoons for mixing, and cake cases. Also a pan of hot water over which to melt the chocolate. Explain that you are going to make some chocolate cakes. Pretend to make these by stirring the unopened packets together. Then, as you all share in the breaking of the chocolate and the wheat, talk about how this has to happen so that they can be made into something even better.

As everyone shares in stirring the wheat into the melted chocolate, point out how the chocolate has to stop being separate squares so it can become warm and melted, ready to join with the wheat and make delicious cakes.

Sometimes we have to give up having a toy all to ourselves, so we can share with someone as friends. Sometimes we have to give up doing what we want to do so that we can let someone else have some fun as well as us.

Giving up what we want to make someone else happy is all part of loving, and every time we do it we get a bit better at it. Whenever we are being loving, we are following Jesus.

Praying

Jesus, you have called me to follow you,
and that's what I want to do.
I'm learning all about loving
because loving is what you do,
and I am following you!

Activities

On the sheet there are pictures of some people following Jesus in different ways. Look at them together and talk about them. How is each person learning to follow Jesus in love? Then they can draw a picture of themselves following Jesus by doing a job God likes them to do. This may be any kind of caring, thoughtful or unselfish behaviour.

Notes

For parents to pray with your child
Jesus, you have called me to follow you, and that's what I want to do.
I'm learning all about loving because loving is what you do and I am following YOU!
How are these people following Jesus?
Here I am following Jesus.
God likes to see me

THIRTEENTH SUNDAY OF THE YEAR

Thought for the day

When we are called to follow Jesus, that means total commitment, with no half-measures.

Readings

1 Kings 19:15, 19-21
Psalm 15
Galatians 5:1, 13-18
Luke 9:51-62

Aim

To understand that we are called to follow Jesus.

Starter

A 'you-do-as-I-do' story. Here is one example. The actions are mostly obvious.

'I'll tell you a story. This story is new,
so you listen carefully and do as I do.
This is Tom Thumb and this is his house.
These are his windows *(hands make glasses at eyes)*
and this is Squeaky, his mouse *(your little finger).*
Early one morning the sun began to shine.
Squeaky mouse sat up in bed and counted up to nine.
One, two, three, four, five, six, seven, eight, nine! *(in a squeaky voice)*
Then he took a great big jump and landed on Tom's bed *(your left hand).*
He quickly ran right up Tom's arm and landed on his head.
Squeaky pulled Tom's hair, Squeaky pulled Tom's nose,
till in the end Tom Thumb jumped up and put on all his clothes.
Then they sat down to breakfast and ate some crusty bread.
And when all that was over, Tom Thumb said . . .'
(back to the beginning)

Teaching

Have several chairs in a line, and prepare beforehand card church windows, door and tower clock as shown below.

By name, ask a particular child to sit on one of the chairs and hold a window. Continue to call by name for particular jobs until you have a complete church. Point out that you called them all to do particular jobs, and in doing them the children have become a church.

Jesus calls his followers to jobs that only we can do, and when we agree, and start doing them, we all become the Church of God. This Church isn't really a building, is it – it's a group of people. And that's what the Church is – a group of people called to do God's work in the world.

Praying

Jesus, you have called me
to follow you,
and here I am!
Lead on, Jesus,
I'm right behind you.

Activities

Have a look at the pictures of some jobs people have been called to and talk about them, and people you know who do such jobs. Then they can draw a picture of themselves doing a job that God likes them to do. This may be any kind of caring, thoughtful behaviour.

Notes

What have these people been called to do?
Who are you following?
Follow the footprints to find him!
This is me following Jesus
To pray with your child
Jesus,
You have called me to follow you, and here I am!
Lead on, Jesus, I'm right behind you.

Fourteenth Sunday of the Year

Thought for the day

In Christ we become a new creation.

Readings

Isaiah 66:10-14
Psalm 65
Galatians 6:14-18
Luke 10:1-12, 17-20

Aim

To know the importance of spreading the good news of God's love.

Starter

Bring with you some postcards you have received from friends on holiday. Show these round, talking together about how nice it is when you hear good news from people who love you enough to let you know about it.

Teaching

Begin by having a time of good news sharing with the group. Then show them a cross (or a number of different ones, from necklace size to a church size one). All these show us the best good news of all – that Jesus is alive and loves us. And we can be good messengers, passing that good news on to the people we meet. We can tell them with our voices and show them by the way we live our lives.

Praying

Lord Jesus, I pray for the people
who do not know you yet
and do not realise that you love us all.
I'd like to be a messenger
and tell them the good news.
Amen.

Activities

On the sheet there is a postcard to make, colour and send with some good news on it. Each child will need a stamp.

Notes

To pray with your child

Lord Jesus,
I pray for the people who
do not know you yet
and do not realise that
you love us all.
I'd like to be a
messenger and tell
them the good news.

We're messengers!

Stick stamp here

Fold and stick to send

Fifteenth Sunday of the Year

Thought for the day

Straighten your lives out and live by God's standards of love.

Readings

Deuteronomy 30:10-4
Psalm 68
Colossians 1:15-20
Luke 10:25-37

Aim

To know the parable of the good neighbour.

Starter

Have a free play session with games such as dressing-up, which encourage the children to play together as well as alongside each other.

Teaching

Tell the story of the good neighbour, involving the children as the characters and helping them act it out. Teach them the summary of the Law to the tune of *London's burning*:

You shall love the
(hands on heart)
Lord your God with
(point upwards)
all your heart and
(hands on heart)
all your mind and
(hold head with hands)
all your strength! All your strength!
(show biceps)
And love your neighbour,
and love your neighbour.
(arms round one another's shoulders)

Praying

Lord Jesus,
with my lips
I can tell you I love you.
With my life
I will show you I love you! Amen.

Activities

The worksheet encourages the children to look at the way people look after others, and there is a picture to finish and colour of the mugged man in the story being looked after by the good Samaritan. Help the children to talk about ways they can be good neighbours.

Notes

What has happened here?

Draw the child being looked after

To pray with your child

**Lord Jesus,
Help me to be kind
and helpful, and use my
strength to make a
better world.
Amen.**

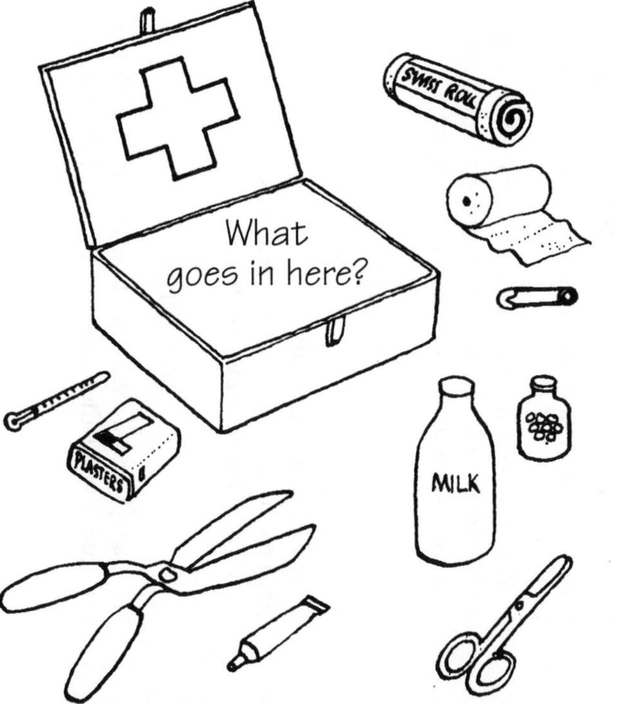

Colour this picture of the man being looked after by a kind person.

Add a

a

and a

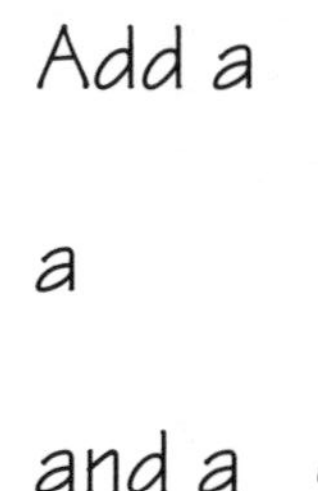

Sixteenth Sunday of the Year

Thought for the day

Attentive listening is all part of serving.

Readings

Genesis 18:1-10
Psalm 14
Colossians 1:24-28
Luke 10:38-42

Aim

To look at the value of listening.

Starter

Play this game in which they have to listen carefully to the instructions. You give them an instruction of where to move to, followed by the way to do it, such as: 'Go to the front wall as aeroplanes; go to the back wall as window cleaners.'

Teaching

Get everyone to find their ears, and talk about what they are for. Try covering and uncovering ears to hear the effect, notice how loud it sounds if you rub your own ear, but if someone else does it to theirs you can hardly hear it at all. Enjoy the gift of hearing and listening that God has given us, and share your favourite sounds. Think about what sounds you hear when you first wake up.

Then do some exercises to train your listening. Sit very still and listen to all the sounds around for a minute, then share what you heard. Whisper something very quietly and see if you can hear it (it might be something funny, or an instruction to touch their toes with their hair). Have a 'news time', with everyone listening carefully to whoever is speaking.

Tell the children about the way all the grown-ups and children used to come out and listen to Jesus, because they found what he said so helpful.

Praying

Thank you, God,
for my ears to listen with.
Help me to get really good at listening
to you and to other people. Amen.

Activities

Have a tape of different sounds and see if the children can guess what they are. On the worksheet there are objects drawn for which they can make the sounds, and the picture of a park encourages them to imagine what sounds they would hear if they were in that place.

Notes

For parents to pray with your child

Thank you God for my ears to listen with. Help me to get really good at listening to you, and to other people. Amen.

If you were here, what would you hear?

Seventeenth Sunday of the Year

Thought for the day

Keep asking for God's Spirit and he will keep pouring out his blessing on you.

Readings

Genesis 18:20-32
Psalm 137
Colossians 2:12-24
Luke 11:1-13

Aim

To know that we can ask God for things, and seek him.

Starter

Play hide and seek, either with people, or hunting for a shoe.

Teaching

Talk about asking for things from our parents. If you asked for some bread, would they give you a stone? If you asked for fish and chips, would they give you snake and chips? If you asked for an egg, would they give you a scorpion? You can laugh together over these, and they will see that although they might look a bit alike, their parents would give them what was good for them, not something that was bad for them. Why? Because their parents love them.

Explain that one day Jesus was teaching the people to pray, and he looked at how good parents are at giving good gifts to the children they love. Well, he said, it's just the same only more so with God. He is a very loving parent to all his children, and we can trust him never to give us anything that would be bad for us.

Jesus wants us to ask him about things, and to ask for his help, and to ask for the things we need. If we ask for something that might not be best for us at the moment, he will probably say, 'No' or 'Not yet'. As we learn to ask for things that he wants for us as well, we shall find that he often says, 'Yes, I'd like that too.' He might even ask our help in getting things done.

Praying

Our Father in heaven,
please give us
all we need today. Amen.

Activities

On the worksheet there are activities to reinforce the asking, seeking and knocking. They can also make a model of an opening and closing door.

Notes

Can you find 6 hidden in this picture?

For parents to pray with your child

Our Father in heaven, please give us all we need today.

Amen.

Cut along the dotted line. Then you can knock and open the door

Eighteenth Sunday of the Year

Thought for the day

True richness is not material wealth; true security is not a financial matter.

Readings

Ecclesiastes 1:2; 2:21-23
Psalm 94
Colossians 3:1-5, 9-11
Luke 12:13-21

Aim

To know that God looks after us like a loving parent looks after a young child.

Starter

If you have a parent who would be willing to bath a baby with the children there, that would be lovely. Or play a matching parents and babies game. Give each child the picture of an animal, and they have to go round the room looking for the baby picture that matches their adult animal.

Teaching

Talk about the different ways in which the people who love us look after us. On the worksheet there are some pictures to start you off. Tell them how God said to his people, 'I love you like that!' Teach them this song, sung to the tune of 'Three blind mice' and putting in all the children's names.

God loves Oliver.
God loves Louise.
God loves Jordan.
God loves Daisy.
He knows when they're friendly
  and when they get mad,
he knows when they're happy
  and when they are sad,
if they help each other it makes him feel glad,
'cos God loves us!

Praying

Dear Jesus,
your love makes me rich.
Thank you for giving me
so much love to love with!

Activities

The worksheet gets the children thinking of three people they love, and drawing what they would like to give them if they could give them anything at all. This will help them to pray for their three people, and help develop their ability to think in out-giving mode. If you have a garden or outside area they can gather some small flowers (daisies, buttercups, dandelions and bindweed are fine) and make a posy of them in wet cotton wool and foil to take into church and lay as thank-offerings in front of the altar. They can take their flowers home with them afterwards.

Notes

God looks after us like a loving parent

Draw what you would like to give three people you love

For
with love

For
with love

For
with love

For parents to pray with your child

**Dear Jesus,
Your love makes me rich.
You are my shepherd, and
so I have all I need.
Amen.**

When we like giving
we are behaving like God.
He likes giving us
good gifts.

You can colour the pictures

Nineteenth Sunday of the Year

Thought for the day

Have faith in God, and get yourself ready to meet him.

Readings

Wisdom 18:6-9
Psalm 32
Hebrews 11:1-2, 8-19
Luke 12:32-48

Aim

To know that God can be trusted.

Starter

Play 'Simon says'. Point out that we had to make sure we only listened to Simon's instructions. We knew if we did that we wouldn't get it wrong.

Teaching

Bring a clock along, with the time an hour fast. Bring one of those pop-up toys which you press down and they suddenly surprise you by popping up before you expected.

As you start, pretend to have just noticed the time on the clock and the time gives you a shock – it's already time we were in church! Then you check with your watch and are very relieved that the clock must be wrong. You know you can trust your watch because you checked that against the television just before you came out.

Talk about there being some things you get to know you can trust, and other things let you down. Share stories about car breakdowns, toys that break, and so on.

We can trust God because he doesn't have 'off' days or go into a sulk. He doesn't move away just when you're getting to know him, and he doesn't go away on holiday. He doesn't have times when you can't get in touch with him. He's always there for us and always fair and loving. So we can trust God with all our fears and our hopes and dreams, all the things that upset us and all the things we're looking forward to. We can trust him with our secrets. He will stay our friend right through to when we're grown up, right to when we get old and even when we've died – he'll still be our friend. By the time we die we will have got to know and love him very well, and he will welcome us into heaven to enjoy being with him for ever.

Praying

Dear Jesus,
it's good to know
I can trust you.
You are always there for me.
Thank you!

Activities

If you can borrow a parachute, you can play some games which build trust and co-operation – working together to make a ball bounce high, and creating a 'mushroom' shape and running underneath it one by one. Or help one another to complete a floor jigsaw. The worksheet gives them space to create a composite picture of themselves and their life, putting in such things as their favourite colours and animals, pastimes and people.

Notes

Dear God, this is me

Draw or stick on things you like – colours, food, and things you like doing

Which could you sit on?

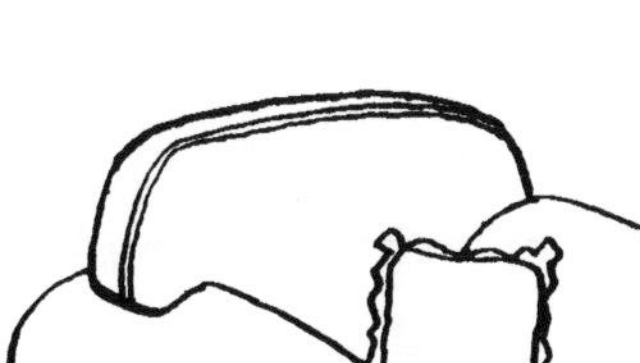

**Dear Jesus,
it's good to know
I can trust you.
You are always
there for me.
Thank you!**

For parents to pray with your child

TWENTIETH SUNDAY OF THE YEAR

Thought for the day

When we fix our eyes on Jesus our lives will reflect his nature.

Readings

Jeremiah 38:4-6, 8-10
Psalm 39
Hebrews 12:1-4
Luke 12:49-53

Aim

To learn that God likes us and wants the best for us.

Starter

Pass the parcel. Make sure everyone has a turn (if necessary, have several parcels with several small groups). Each layer contains a freezer label with 'I'm special' written on it. Eventually every child is wearing one.

Teaching

Pass round a flower each for the children to hold, and talk together about what it is like – what its petals and leaves look like, what it smells and feels like, and so on. Marvel over all the care that God has taken in bringing a flower like this into being.

Now pass round something else to enjoy and notice, such as feathers, stones or vegetables. Again draw their attention to all the care God has taken over these things.

Collect everything in and say we've got another collection of beautiful, amazing things God has made. Get everyone to stand up in the circle and hold hands. At the moment they are making a sort of chain, but they aren't daisies. At the moment they are quiet, but they can speak. What – or who – can they be? It's us!

Sit everyone down and go round the group picking out one nice thing about everyone, and then enthuse together over the loving care God has taken over each one of us. No wonder God likes us and thinks us all very special.

Praying

Thank you, God,
for making me
and knowing me
and liking me.
It's special being special!

Activities

Make finger-print pictures, using shallow trays of paint and hand-washing bowls between colours. Some suggestions for making their prints into people and objects are given on the worksheet.

Notes

Why is this day special

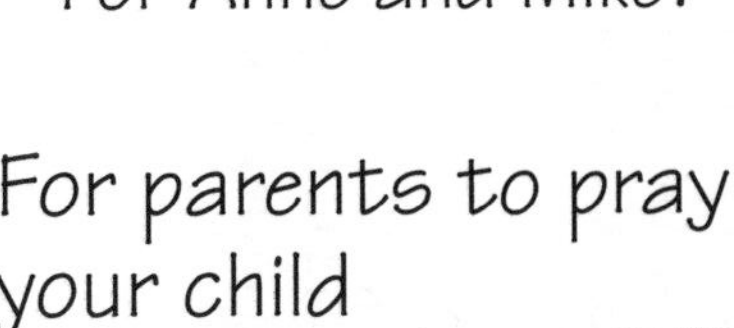

For Anne and Mike?

Why is this day special for Oliver?

Some ideas

For parents to pray with your child

Thank you God for making me and knowing me and liking me. It's special - being special!

This is me on my special day

My finger-print picture

TWENTY-FIRST SUNDAY OF THE YEAR

Thought for the day

At the great and final gathering-in, it will be a question of each person's chosen life direction, and each response to the way of God.

Readings

Isaiah 66:18-21
Psalm 116
Hebrews 12:5-7, 11-13
Luke 13:22-30

Aim

To know that God teaches us to love, and looks after us when we make mistakes.

Starter

Share each other's stories of times when we have been frightened or scared, and what helped us to be brave.

Teaching

Sometimes we have to do things which are frightening or which hurt. Some people don't like taking medicine, but we know we have to take it if we are ill, so that we get better. We have injections (which aren't much fun) because they are good for us and stop us getting ill. Sometimes our mums and dads make us sit still and quiet so that the other people in the family can watch a programme they like.

All through our lives we are learning, and sometimes the learning gives us bumps and bruises (like when we fall off our bikes or graze our knees).

God has given us a whole lifetime to spend, with a wonderful world to live in, and our job is to learn how to love. We start learning this as soon as we are born and we go on learning it till we die. And sometimes it hurts. But our God is always there with us, helping us learn, and comforting us when we make mistakes. It is God who teaches us how to love, and every time you find yourself not wanting to be kind and helpful and thoughtful, that's when you are being given your practice to do. It is hard to be loving when we don't want to be, and we need all the practice we can get.

Praying

Lord God, thank you for loving us
and giving us such a good world to live in.
Teach us how to live good and loving lives.
Amen.

Activities

On the sheet they can recognise objects based on the clues which leaders read out to them, and they can play a 'Bingo' type game, looking in a picture for people being given practice in loving. When they spot some forgiving or sharing going on, they place a counter or a card shape over the square until all six counters are on the picture, making the Jesus sign of love – a cross.

Notes

1. It is pointed
2. You can break it
3. You can sharpen it
4. You can draw with it

WHAT IS IT?

1. You can eat it
2. It tastes nice on toast
3 It comes out of a shell
4. It was laid by a hen

For parents to pray with your child

Lord God,
thank you for loving us
and giving us such a
good world to live in.
Teach us how to live
good and loving lives.
Amen.

Twenty-second Sunday of the Year

Thought for the day

When we live God's way, both individually and as a community, we will be greatly blessed.

Readings

Ecclesiasticus 3:17-20, 28-29
Psalm 67
Hebrews 12:18-19, 22-24
Luke 14:1, 7-14

Aim

To know the story of the guests choosing the most important seats.

Starter

While the music plays, pass round a grand hat or a crown. Whenever the music stops, whoever is wearing the hat or crown stands up, and all the others bow and curtsey to them, saying, 'Yes, your majesty; no, your majesty!'

Teaching

You can either use puppets to tell the story today, or an assortment of character toys, some of which are very new and posh, while others are well loved, old and tatty. Lay a low table with a cloth and plates of drawn food, and arrange all the chairs around it. One by one the characters come in, talking to themselves about the party, and admiring the food.

One of the new, posh ones looks to see which the most important seat is, and decides to sit there because they are *so important.*

One of the old and tatty well-loved ones comes and looks for the lowest, least important seat, because they are conscious of being old and worn, and not very grand.

When the host comes in they go to the old, worn one and give him a big hug, really pleased that he has been able to come to the party. They ask him to come up and sit with them at the top of the table, as he's so important, having been such a good friend for years. When they get to the top of the table the hosts find the posh guest sitting there and ask them to move down so their special guest can sit there instead. The posh guest voices her embarrassment as she moves down and the old worn one takes his place at the top of the table.

This story teaches us not to think we're far more important than anyone else and deserve better than anyone else. Instead of rushing for the best place, or the biggest cake, or the first go, sometimes we need to enjoy giving the best to other people.

Praying

Big and small,
short and tall,
you made us all,
you love us all! Amen.

Activities

On the worksheet the children are putting the guests in the right places, and the food on the plates. Also, they can paint or model some food on a paper plate to remind them of the story. Today's prayer can be written out on the back of the plate.

Notes

Colour the guests, cut them out and stick them at the right place for the party. Draw in their food.

Jesus invites us to be his friends

For parents to pray with your child

Big and small
short and tall
you made us all,
you love us all!
Amen.

Twenty-third Sunday of the Year

Thought for the day

Following Jesus is expensive – it costs everything, but it's worth it.

Readings

Wisdom 9:13-18
Psalm 89
Philemon 9-10, 12-17
Luke 14:25-33

Aim

To know that it is worth the cost to follow Jesus.

Starter

Play shops, with play money, boxes and cartons, cut-out fruit and some paper bags.

Teaching

Talk about going shopping, and what they like buying and what they don't like buying. Talk about how we sometimes see things we would like, but we can't have them because they cost too much.

Tell the story, with the aid of a few appropriate props, of a child who sees a toy she really loves and would like for her birthday. Her mum tells her that she won't be able to have it as it costs too much money. The child keeps thinking about the toy, and decides she wants it so much that she doesn't mind not having any other presents, and no birthday treat, if that means she can have it. Her mum and dad talk it over with her. They don't want her to choose to do without those things and then be upset when she has only got one toy. The child is certain that this toy is worth it, so her mum and dad arrange for her to have the toy she wants so much. And the child is so happy with this one thing that she doesn't mind having no other presents and no birthday treat.

Following Jesus is really wonderful. It's wonderful having Jesus as our friend and knowing he loves us all the way through our life and wherever we travel to. But when we follow Jesus, we choose to do without some things.

We choose to do without being selfish, even when we want to be. We choose to do without being unkind, even when we feel grumpy. We choose to do without wanting things all the time, even if we like them.

But it's worth doing without these nasty things, because being with Jesus makes us so happy.

Praying

Jesus, I love you
and I will live like you,
even when it is easier not to. Amen.

Activities

On the worksheet there is a picture to colour of Jesus with the children, and the children can draw themselves in the picture.

Notes

Match real money with these coins, and make rubbings of some real coins, too.

For parents to pray with your child

Jesus, I love you and I will live like you even when it's easier not to.

Amen.

Twenty-fourth Sunday of the Year

Thought for the day

Jesus does not avoid the company of sinners but befriends them.

Readings

Exodus 32:7-11, 13-14
Psalm 50
1 Timothy 1:12-17
Luke 15:1-32

Aim

To know the story of the good shepherd and the lost sheep.

Starter

Hide and seek, using a model sheep.

Teaching

Let the children help make a landscape from upturned bowls draped with a green sheet or towel. Use model sheep, either plastic ones or home-made from thin card and cotton wool. Bushes and shrubs can be small house plants in pots, such as spider plants and money trees.

When the landscape is set up, tell the story, moving the sheep around as you talk about the normal daily routine for the shepherd caring for his flock, and the lost sheep being found and brought safely home.

Praying

Good shepherd,
thank you for looking after us.
Help us to look after each other. Amen.

Activities

The children can make sheep masks using the instructions on the worksheet, and search for lost sheep in a picture which can then be coloured in.

Notes

How to make a sheep mask

cotton wool
cut out
punch hole
cut
paper plate
cut along here

Cut shape from a paper plate; draw on the face, cut eye holes and stick on cotton wool. Secure round the head with wool.

To pray with your child

**Good shepherd,
thank you for looking
after us.
Help us to look after
each other.
Amen.**

Can you find the lost sheep? How will the shepherd get to it?
Colour the picture

Twenty-fifth Sunday of the Year

Thought for the day

If you cannot be trusted with worldly riches, or even small amounts of money, then you will not be trusted with spiritual riches either.

Readings

Amos 8:4-7
Psalm 112
1 Timothy 2:1-8
Luke 16:1-13

Aim

To learn that we are to be good 'caretakers' and look after things as well as people.

Starter

A potato and spoon game. For each small group of children (2-4 in a group), place a bowl at each end of the room. In one of the bowls there is a potato and a spoon. The first person carries the potato in the spoon from one bowl to the other. The next carries it back to the first bowl, and so on. They can all have two turns. This can either be competitive or simply an activity which several groups happen to be playing at the same time, depending on the age of the children.

Teaching

Talk about how careful they all had to be to walk along holding the potato in the spoon without it falling off. Think how careful we have to be carrying a bowl of cereal, or a drink of juice. We have to really think about what we are doing. If we start thinking about something else, we can end up spilling it all over the floor!

Jesus told his friends that God takes great care making us and looking after us, and he wants us to take great care of things as well. Show a picture of different age groups working or playing together. He wants us to look after one another. (How?) Show a globe. He wants us to look after our world. (How?) Show a toy and a jacket. And he wants us to look after any things we are given to use or play with. (How?)

Praying

Dear God,
thank you for all the things I have been given
to use and to play with.
Help me to look after them well
and be ready to share them with others. Amen.

Activities

There is space on the sheet for the children to draw the things to use and to play with that they like most, and some pictures of things being looked after well and badly, so they can develop their understanding of what good stewardship means.

Notes

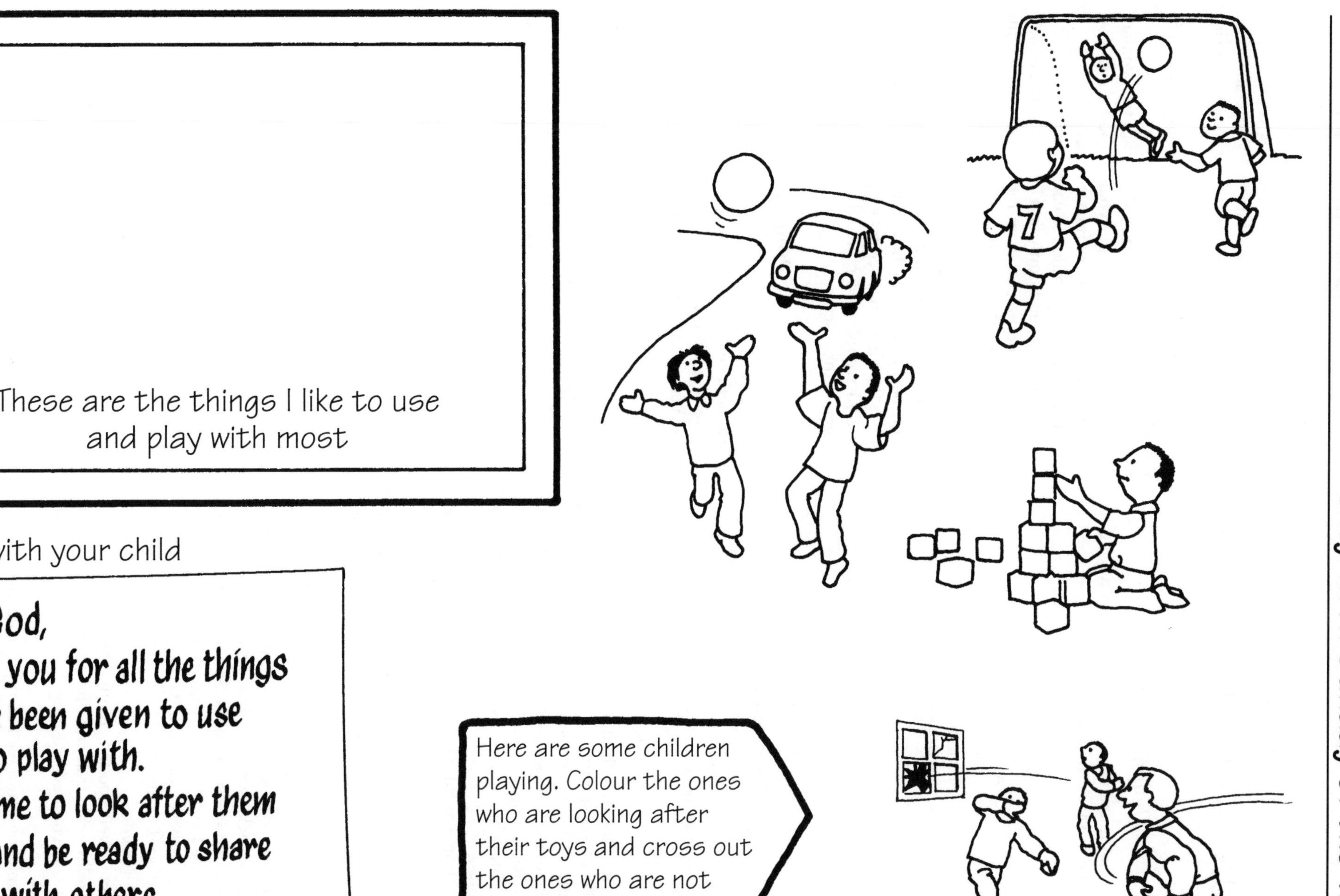

Here are some children playing. Colour the ones who are looking after their toys and cross out the ones who are not

These are the things I like to use and play with most

To pray with your child

**Dear God,
thank you for all the things
I have been given to use
and to play with.
Help me to look after them
well and be ready to share
them with others.
Amen.**

Twenty-sixth Sunday of the Year

Thought for the day

Wealth can make us complacent so that we fail to notice the needs of those around us.

Readings

Amos 6:1a, 4-7
Psalm 145
1 Timothy 6:11-16
Luke 16:19-31

Aim

To know that we are to notice one another's needs.

Starter

Spot the difference. The children hide their eyes while you change something (you might take a shoe off, or swap your watch to the other wrist) and then they have to guess what is different.

Teaching

Tell a story about a child noticing someone's need. Here is one possibility:

Emily and her dad were doing the shopping. It was the big weekly shop in the supermarket to get things like toothpaste, cocoa-pops, toilet paper and bread. Emily had got the list, and Dad was pushing the trolley.

The shop was full of people, some of them filling plastic bags with apples and potatoes, and others trying to work out the cheapest way to buy cheese. They were so busy with what they were choosing to buy that no one noticed a sticky white line on the floor by the cat food.

At least, nearly no one noticed. Emily saw it and wondered what it was. As she went to find the rabbit and chicken flavour (her cat's favourite) she followed the sticky white trail, and smelt the smell of concentrated washing liquid. So that's what it was! Emily could see the trail disappearing round the corner into the lemonade and coke part of the shop.

'Dad!' said Emily. 'Look!'

Dad looked.

'Mmm, well spotted, Emily,' he said. 'We had better follow that trail and find out why it's there.'

'It's concentrated washing liquid I think,' said Emily.

'I think you could well be right,' said Dad.

They pushed their trolley round the corner. There, just between the large bottles of lime and lemon and the small bottles of blackcurrant and apple was a woman pushing a trolley. And on the front of the trolley was a refill of concentrated washing liquid, leaking white sticky stuff along the floor as the trolley went along. Anyone could slip over on it and hurt themselves.

Emily and her dad showed the woman the white sticky trail.

'Oh good heavens, fancy that!' said the woman. 'Fancy me not noticing! What a good thing you noticed it before anyone hurt themselves.'

Dad and Emily smiled at each other.

The woman and Emily and her dad told the shop assistants and helped them mop up the mess with paper towels. The manager put down some orange cones saying 'Wet floor' on them, so people would know it wasn't safe to walk there yet.

Talk about how good it was that Emily noticed, and share any stories the children want to tell about times they have noticed when people need help.

God wants us to notice things and be ready to come to the rescue.

Praying

Dear God,
use our eyes
to see the needs around us
and use our hands to help. Amen.

Activities

On the sheet there is a picture on which to spot various needs, and a pair of glasses to make.

Notes

What do they need?
Sport
CRISPS
How could we help?
To pray with your child
Dear God,
use our eyes to
see the needs around us
and use our hands
to help.
Amen.
Can you make some
pipe-cleaner glasses?
These are the hands I mean!

TWENTY-SEVENTH SUNDAY OF THE YEAR

Thought for the day

God hears our distress and our crying, and feels it with us.

Readings

Habakkuk 1:2-3; 2:2-4
Psalm 94
2 Timothy 1:6-8, 13-14
Luke 17:5-10

Aim

To learn about perseverance.

Starter

Have some buckets and beanbags, so the children can try throwing the beanbags into the buckets.

Teaching

Make up an obstacle course which a soft toy, such as a bear, could negotiate with a bit of help from his friends. This might include something high to balance along, a dark tunnel he must hurry through on his own, and something to climb up.

Make a bear walk the obstacle course, talking to himself in a growly voice as he goes along. He is sometimes scared and anxious by the height, sometimes frightened and sad about being alone in the dark, and sometimes finding it all an uphill struggle. There are also parts of his journey with fun and excitement and good views. Through all the difficult parts the bear bravely perseveres. The children can applaud him when he eventually reaches the end of the course.

Talk about how the bear kept on going, even when he was scared or tired. That's what God wants us to do in life.

Praying

Make a ring of string which everyone holds and passes through their hands as they pray:
Lord, help me to keep trying
again and again and again!
Lord, help me to keep loving
on and on and on. Amen.

Activities

On the worksheet there is an obstacle course for the children to make their fingers walk along, and a 'keeping on and on' game to make, for which they will need string.

Notes

Start
To pray with your child
Lord, help me to keep trying,
again and again and again!
Lord, help me to keep loving,
on and on and on!
Amen.
Get some
Cut it
Tie it
Fix on a flag
Make your flag go up and down
Well done!

Twenty-eighth Sunday of the Year

Thought for the day

God can always use even seemingly hopeless situations for good.

Readings

2 Kings 5:14-17
Psalm 97
2 Timothy 2:8-13
Luke 17:11-19

Aim

To know that Jesus healed the ten lepers and one said 'thank you'.

Starter

Provide a selection of sorting-out games and toys, such as building something from a jumble of bricks or boxes, putting shapes in the right holes, and jigsaw puzzles. Today we are going to look at the way Jesus sorted out ten problems all at once!

Teaching

Using the carpet tiles surface, tell the story of today's Gospel. You will need cut-outs of the lepers, a distant village, some trees, Jesus, the priest, and the leper who said 'thank you'. You can base them on the pictures below. The road to the village can either be a cloth, or strip of paper.

Praying

When we are sad *(chin in hands)*,
you cheer us up *(trace big smile with finger)*.
When we cry *(fists in eyes)*,
you brush our tears away *(brush face with hands)*.
When we feel weak *(go droopy)*,
you make us strong *(show muscles)*
and we say THANK YOU! *(shout)*

Activities

There is a picture of the lepers throwing off their bandages happily when they are healed which the children can colour, after they have counted the lepers and various other things.

Notes

To pray with your child

When we are sad (chin in hands)
you cheer us up (trace big smile with finger)
When we cry (fists in eyes)
you brush our tears away (brush face with hands)
When we feel weak (go droopy)
you make us strong (show muscles)
and we say:

THANK YOU!

How many?

People who said 'thank you'

Here I am saying 'THANK YOU'

Twenty-ninth Sunday of the Year

Thought for the day

Don't get side-tracked; always pray and don't give up.

Readings

Exodus 17:8-13
Psalm 120
2 Timothy 3:14-4:2
Luke 18:1-8

Aim

To look at the value of regular prayer.

Starter

Here we go round the mulberry bush. With one of the regular morning jobs being: 'This is the way we pray to God on a cold and frosty morning'.

Teaching

Bring a large circle of card split into the four seasons, and a circular band of paper showing the regular events of a day, based on the pictures below.

Turn the chart round like a wheel, and talk about the seasons and the way the same thing happens every year. Then point out that the days all have a pattern as well. Move the band round so that they can see the same pictures coming up day after day. There are some things we do every day.

Jesus tells us that we should make praying part of our daily pattern too. Have the praying picture, and stick it on the band in the morning, before eating, and before sleeping. Then turn the whole thing round a few times so they get the idea of the ongoing pattern.

Praying

When I wake up I say:
Good morning, Jesus!
Help me live your way today.
When I sit down to eat I say:
Thank you for this food.
Before I go to sleep I say:
Goodnight, Jesus.
Thank you for looking after me.

Activities

The worksheet helps them make their own day's band to use, and there is some pictorial teaching on how to pray.

Notes

Cut along here

God loves us all day and all night

Cut along here

To pray with your child

When I wake up I say:

Good morning, Jesus!
Help me live your way today.

When I sit down to eat I say:

Thank you for this food.

Before I go to sleep I say:

Goodnight, Jesus.
Thank you for looking after me.

Draw in what you do each day. Colour all the pictures. Cut the strip out and stick the ends together

What can I say when I pray?

You can praise God, who made us all

You can thank God for your life

You can enjoy being with him

Thirtieth Sunday of the Year

Thought for the day

When we recognise our dependence on God we will approach him with true humility and accept his gifts with joy.

Readings

Ecclesiasticus 35:12-14, 16-17
Psalm 33
2 Timothy 4:6-8, 16-18
Luke 18:9-14

Aim

To know that we are to let God into our life as the earth lets in water.

Starter

Play with water and have lots of sponges, so they can try transferring water from one container to another using the sponges' soaking and water-holding quality.

Teaching

Have a tray of dry earth, and point out how nothing will grow in it if it stays as dry as this all the time, because things need water to grow. We can't grow any goodness in our lives if we don't get showered with God's love.

But that's all right, because God is always there showering us with his love. As you talk, shower the earth with a watering can. He gives us a beautiful world to live in, fruits and vegetables and animals and families to enjoy and look after. He gives us life, and minds to think with, and bodies to move around with.

All the time we keep ourselves open to God like this earth is open to the water, he can fill our lives with his love and we will grow more and more loving and truthful and good.

Praying

Thank you, God,
for the rain that falls.

(make fingers into falling rain)

Thank you for trees
that grow so tall.

(stretch up)

Thank you for this life
you have given us all!

(move and dance about)

Activities

Use the wet earth to plant some bulbs to be ready in the spring. The worksheet has a picture to colour and add the raindrops. Provide raindrops cut from shiny blue and silver wrapping paper for this.

Notes

Stick on the raindrops

Can you see

- 6 trees
- 10 apples
- 1 river
- 2 clouds
- 1 tractor

To pray with your child

Thank you, God,
for the rain that falls. (make fingers into falling rain)
Thank you for trees that grow so tall. (stretch up)
Thank you for this life you have given us all! (move and dance about)

Thirty-first Sunday of the Year

Thought for the day

Jesus came to search out the lost and save them. Through him we come to our senses and make our lives clean.

Readings

Wisdom 11:22-12:2
Psalm 144
2 Thessalonians 1:11-2:2
Luke 19:1-10

Aim

To be introduced to the story of Zacchaeus.

Starter

Spot the birds. Fix a number of bird pictures high up around the room. Show the children an example of what they are looking for, and set them off hunting for the pictures, but don't tell them they will have to look up to see them. Let them discover that for themselves.

Teaching

Prepare the tree by fixing a card or thick paper tree outline to a chair, so that when Zacchaeus stands on the chair you can just see his face over the top of the tree. Give Jesus and Zacchaeus head-dresses to wear, and have all the other children standing at the side of the road as Jesus comes walking through their village. Let Zacchaeus lead Jesus and his friends across the room to his house (some chairs can make the walls) where they sit down to eat. Then they can come outside for Zacchaeus to announce to all the people waiting outside that he is changing his life. He's going to stop cheating people out of their money, and pay back all his debts four times over. All the people can give him three cheers and a round of applause.

Point out that although Zacchaeus was short, he wasn't too short to work with God. They may be short, but they are not too short or too young to work with God either.

Praying

Look, Lord,
I may be short
but I am not too short
to be your friend.
I want to be in your team
and work with you today.

Activities

They can all make a tall tree with Zacchaeus in it to remind them of the story. You will need a length of wallpaper for each child, cut into a trunk, and the tree's crown.

Notes

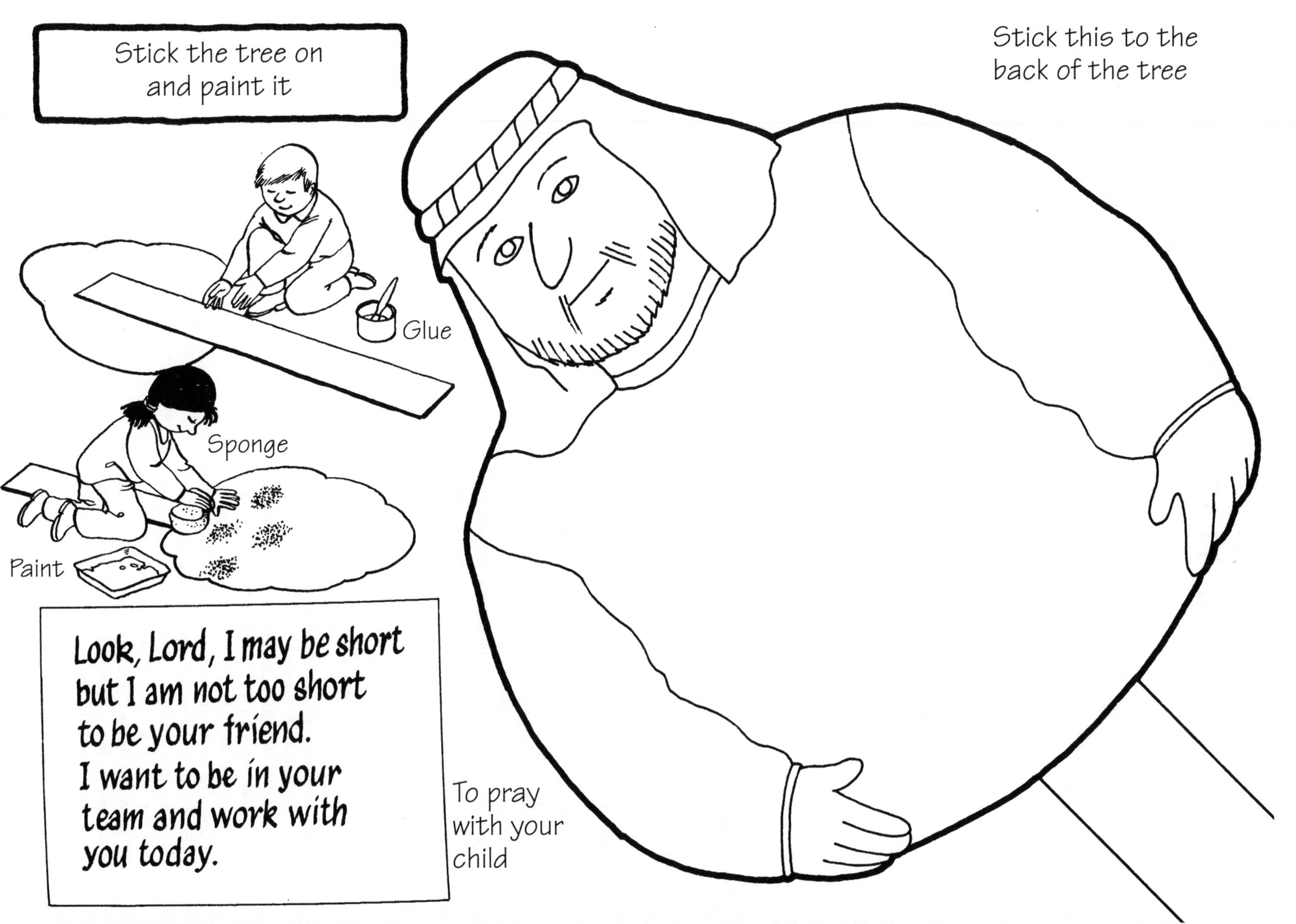
Stick the tree on and paint it
Stick this to the back of the tree
Glue
Sponge
Paint
Look, Lord, I may be short
but I am not too short
to be your friend.
I want to be in your
team and work with
you today.
To pray with your child

Thirty-second Sunday of the Year

Thought for the day

Life after death is not wishful thinking but a definite reality.

Readings

Maccabees 7:1-2, 9-14
Psalm 16
2 Thessalonians 2:16-3:5
Luke 20:27-38

Aim

To know that Jesus told us life goes on after death.

Starter

Place some tiny cakes decorated with chocolate drops in a box or tin, and have an extra packet of chocolate drops with you. Tell the children that there is something nice in the tin. Can they see it, without taking off the lid? No. Do they trust you to tell them the truth? (I wonder!) Do they believe that there really is something nice in the tin?

Assure them that there really is something nice in it, and you are going to give them a little idea of what it is like. Now give each child a chocolate drop to enjoy. What do they think is in the tin? Well, it's certainly something to do with chocolate drops. Open the tin so they can all see. It's like chocolate drops but even better, because there's a whole cake, decorated with a chocolate drop for everyone. Now you can give them out one by one, so that everyone has one.

Teaching

When Jesus was walking about on our earth he told his friends that life goes on after our bodies wear out and die. He told them heaven was a nice place to be, and they would be very happy there. (As you say this, hold the closed tin.)

Can we trust Jesus to tell us the truth? Yes, we can.

So if Jesus said there is life after we die, and people are happy there, can we believe him? Yes, we can.

What will it be like? (Pick up the empty packet of chocolate drops.) Jesus gives his friends some clues, and he lets us feel the joy and happiness and peace and love of heaven sometimes. Heaven will be like that only much, much better!

Praying

Be near me, Lord Jesus, I ask thee to stay
close by me for ever and love me I pray.
Bless all the dear children in thy tender care
and fit us for heaven to live with thee there.

Activities

There is a dot-to-dot angel to complete, and then they can draw and paint heaven in their favourite colours. If you want to make this a collage picture, bring along an assortment of different colours and textures for them to use.

Notes

Heaven goes on and on and on

To pray with your child

**Be near me, Lord Jesus,
I ask thee to stay close
by me for ever and love
me I pray. Bless all the
dear children in thy tender
care and fit us for heaven
to live with thee there.**

I think heaven might look like this

Thirty-third Sunday of the Year

Thought for the day

There will be dark and dangerous times as the end approaches, but by standing firm through it all we will gain life.

Readings

Malachi 3:19-20
Psalm 97
2 Thessalonians 3:7-12
Luke 21:5-19

Aim

To know that God is a fair judge.

Starter

Weighing and sorting games, using lots of different items, such as stones, vegetables, pasta, bricks, saucepans and feathers. Sort according to shape, use or colour. Use balance scales, or hang two baskets at either end of a broom handle and hold it in the middle. The children can try to balance the baskets.

Teaching

Using toys or puppets, act out several situations which are not fair. Tell the children to shout out 'That's not fair!' as soon as they spot something which isn't. Then talk about why it isn't fair, and act out the same situation, this time making it fair. Here are some ideas for situations:

- Three sweets are shared out between three toys with one toy having two sweets and one having none.
- It's clearing-up time and one toy is allowed to carry on reading while the others have to do all the tidying up on their own.
- The toys are playing 'catch' and one says he hasn't been caught when really he has.

Our God always judges justly, or fairly. He always knows both sides of the story, and he is always fair. So we can trust him.

God has made us able to tell what is fair, so that we can play fairly and grow wise, choosing to do what is right and just. God wants us to stand up for what is fair. He doesn't want people to treat each other badly and unfairly.

Praying

Dear God,
you are a good judge.
You are always fair.
Help me to be fair as well.

Activities

They can make their own set of balances to use at home. They will each need two yoghurt pots, wool, and half a pea stick. The worksheet gives instructions.

Notes

How to make a pair of SCALES
You will need:
2 yoghurt pots
2 lengths of wool
a pea stick
1. Tie the ends of the wool to the pots to make a handle
2. Loop the handles over the ends of the peastick and tape them down
3. Hold the stick in the middle. You can now share things out so they are fair
To pray with your child
Dear God,
you are a good judge.
You are always fair.
Help me to be fair as well.
Share the cakes out so it is fair

CHRIST THE KING

Thought for the day

This Jesus, dying by crucifixion between criminals, is the anointed King of all creation in whom all things are reconciled.

Readings

2 Samuel 5:1-3
Psalm 121
Colossians 1:11-20
Luke 23:35-43

Aim

To know and celebrate that Jesus is our King.

Starter

Scatter different coloured and named circles all over the floor, one for each person. Everyone starts by standing on their own circle. When the music starts, everyone moves and dances around. When the music stops, they go and stand on their spot. A matching set of named circles (small ones) are in a basket, and one is drawn and that person is given a crown to wear. When the music starts this time, everyone follows what the King or Queen does. The crown is changed each time the music stops, and you can easily give everyone a go by removing their name from the basket once it has been chosen.

Teaching

Hold the crown and talk about what kings are often like in fairy stories, establishing that they are usually the most important person in the kingdom, with lots of power and lots of money.

As Christians, we belong to a kingdom. It's a kingdom of love and joy and peace and goodness and forgiveness. Anyone in any country can be part of this kingdom, if they ask to be. It's a kingdom which grows bigger and bigger as more people get to meet with God. And our King is someone who was born in a stable, and died on a cross, and came back to life again. Do you know his name? Yes, it's Jesus. And if we are part of the family of God, which we are, that means we are princes and princesses in the kingdom of God!

Praying

Dear Jesus,
you are my friend
and yet you are a King!
I am glad I live
in your kingdom.

Activities

The worksheet can be decorated and turned into a crown, which the children can wear as they sing some songs to celebrate, such as:

- *Who's the king of the jungle?*
- *I rejoice in making Jesus happy*
- *I'm H - A - P - P - Y*
- *If you're happy and you know it*

Notes

cut
Dear Jesus, you are my friend and
yet you are a King!
I am glad I live in your kingdom.
cut
Jesus is my friend and my king
signed
cut